Every Sun That Rises

WYATT MOORE

of Caddo Lake

Including "Building the Last Caddo Bateau"

Edited by Thad Sitton and James H. Conrad
Photographs by Stan Godwin and Jim Cammack

UNIVERSITY OF TEXAS PRESS
AUSTIN

First edition, 1985

Requests for permission to reproduce material from
this work should be sent to: Permissions, University of Texas Press,
Box 7819, Austin, Texas 78713.

LIBRARY OF CONGRESS CATALOGING-IN-PUBLICATION DATA
Moore, Wyatt A. 1901–
Every sun that rises.
  Bibliography: p.
  Includes index.
  1. Moore, Wyatt A., 1901– . 2. Caddo Lake
Region (La. and Tex.)—Biography. 3. Caddo Lake
Region (La. and Tex.)—Social life and customs.
I. Sitton, Thad, 1941–   II. Conrad, James H.
III. Title.
F392.C17M666 1985   976.3'99   85-11175
ISBN 0-292-71007-7
ISBN 0-292-71108-5 (pbk.)

To the Raconteurs

Contents

AFRICAN QUEEN under a full head of steam, 1975.

Every Sun That Rises

WYATT MOORE

of Caddo Lake

I decline to accept the end of man. It is easy enough to say that man is immortal simply because he will endure: that when the last ding-dong of doom has clanged and faded from the last worthless rock hanging tideless in the last red and dying evening, that even then there will still be one more sound: that of his puny inexhaustible voice, still talking.

WILLIAM FAULKNER
(Nobel Prize Acceptance Speech, Stockholm, Sweden, 1950)

Introduction

Wyatt A. Moore, who once told us, "What I done and what I been accused of covers everything, you put 'em both together," was born in 1901 at Karnack, Texas. He exaggerates, but perhaps not very much. In over eighty years at Caddo Lake, Moore has been boat operator, commercial fisherman, boatbuilder, farmer, fishing and hunting camp operator, guide, commercial hunter, trapper, raftsman, moonshiner, oil field worker, water well driller, and mechanical jack of all trades. Moore often pursued several of these occupations simultaneously and still found time for his lifelong study of the natural and human history of Caddo Lake, a vast, wooded swamp lake as little known to most Texans as the Brooks Range of Alaska.

Every Sun That Rises is Moore's story, transcribed and edited from his own spoken words. It is also the first fruits of the Caddo Lake Oral History Project, an enterprise which itself began with an encounter with Wyatt Moore.

Others have discovered Moore before and since. A decade ago the editors of *National Geographic* hired him to guide their photographers around Caddo Lake. Focusing on one or another of his occupations—Moore as boatbuilder, moonshiner, oil field rigger, etc.—quite a number of newspaper feature writers, film makers, and folklorists have visited him across the years, and few have gone away disappointed. Most recently, author James Michener visited Moore to solicit his opinion about the probable locations of early-day plantations around Caddo Lake, and Bill Moyers made him the star of a fifteen-minute segment of "Marshall, Texas, Marshall, Texas," the opening program of his "A Walk through the Twentieth Century" TV series.

Moore is, as one East Texas folklorist said, "a real pistol." Writers, film makers, folklorists, and now oral historians have sought him out, and all have come away with excellent grist for their respective mills. In the pages that follow, readers will come to know Moore

as skilled raconteur, laconic wit, and—perhaps most character-
istically—keen historical interpreter of his strange homeland of
Caddo Lake.

Twenty-three miles long, some forty-thousand acres at high water,
stretching across two Texas counties and one Louisiana parish, Caddo
is the second-largest natural lake in the American South. It is also
the most productive freshwater lake in Texas, with no less than
seventy-one fish species present within its waters.[1] Since the first
decade of this century, Caddo's level has been artificially maintained by a low dam in the vicinity of Mooringsport, Louisiana.
Properly lake-like at the Louisiana end, open water merges into a
labyrinthine swamp on the Texas side. Open stretches alternate
with moss-draped cypress brakes and "islands"; lily-pad meadows
stretch into shimmering distances; obscure bayous and boat channels twist and turn upon themselves through a maze of aquatic vegetation. The plants are yonquapin and spatterdock, duckweed, golden
club, water hyacinth, and water lily.

At the edges of the lake (and Caddo has many scores of miles of
internal edges as well as external ones), open water gradually merges
into swamp, a swamp zone that is extending over more and more of
the area as time goes by. A few decades ago, great floods would sweep
down the drainage of Big Cypress Bayou which feeds Caddo, bringing
water levels over fifteen feet higher than at present, scouring channels clean and washing away water vegetation over large areas. In the
intervals between floods the swamp vegetation would reassert itself,
covering open areas and infringing on channels. Now, dams on Big
Cypress and its tributaries permanently control such floods. The
scouring action of high water is much less, and the relative clarity of
the waters coming down (sediments being trapped by the reservoirs)
further encourages photosynthesis and the growth of water plants.
Year by year, the vegetable empire of the swamp advances at the expense of open lake, and Caddo becomes even more of an aquatic
maze. Tourists stick to the marked boat trails, well aware that even
modest detours into the swamp may lead to "a night in the Caddo
Motel." Only Moore, a few other old-timers, and such latter-day lake
explorers as Moore's friend Paul Ray Martin know large areas of the
lake well enough to move freely across its inner recesses. U.S. Geological Survey and tourist maps prove poor guides to the real com-
plexities of the Texas end of Caddo, but such maps do mark many
places that few know how to find these days. Goat Island, Pig Turd

---

1. Joe E. Toole, "The Biology of Caddo Lake" (paper delivered to the
Greater Caddo Lake Association, November 1983).

Island, Gravier Slough, Back Lake, Whistleberry Slough, Eagle's Nest, Devil's Elbow, Red Belly, Turtle Shell, Whangdoodle Pass, the Judd Hole—these and other place names punctuate the labyrinth, their origins obscure, lost reminders of the days of steamboats and the old bateau men.

The Judd Hole is named for Old Man Judd, a wild old man who camped out at a remote place on Clinton's Lake and ultimately died there, one of many "lake rats" and outlaws who have made Caddo their home. Wyatt Moore knew Old Man Judd, and the Judd Hole is part of his intricate mental map of Caddo Lake. Much of the history of Caddo remains undocumented and unwritten, and Moore by virtue of a lifelong interest in his home place has made himself a walking library of the "back history" of Caddo Lake. His many occupations have taken him into almost every nook and corner of the great lake, and wherever he has gone, whatever he has done, he has sought to learn more about his subject. Since the history of Caddo Lake was, and is, more in living memory than anywhere else, Moore says that he has always "tried to talk to people who I thought were smarter than I was." Even in his youth he sought out old men and women down dusty roads to learn what they could tell him about early times on the lake.

Now, in his eighties himself, Moore has become a living repository of the remembered history of Caddo, gleaned from the minds of other old-timers across all those years. His mental library is a little disorderly, but enormously detailed and colorful. He tells of the strange and conjectural origins of Caddo Lake, of its relationships to the Neutral Ground, or "Texas Badlands," and of the days from his mother's childhood when the great steamboats still walked the lake. Some of that earlier history of Caddo should be explored before Moore is left to tell his personal story.

When, and how, did Caddo Lake come into existence? The most likely theory is that the lake was created around 1800 by the Great Raft, a logjam of monumental proportions caused by the action of the Red River in its alluvial floodplain.[2]

Great masses of timber washed downstream to become part of this vast logjam, which was well over one-hundred miles long and stretched from Natchitoches, Louisiana, to Hurricane Bluffs, north of Shreveport. The Great Raft filled the channel of the Red River from bank to bank. It was intermittent rather than continuous, with dead-water pools covered with lily pads between the major logjams.

2. Frank D. Smith, "Caddo Lake" (unpublished paper, Caddo Lake Oral History Project, East Texas State University, Commerce), p. 5.

At these logjams the raft was a solid mass, with trunks stacked twenty-five feet high bonded together by roots, moss, and decades of cemented silt. Downstream, older portions tended to decay and disintegrate, while the upper section grew gradually upstream as spring floods brought down additional trees and other debris from the river's caving banks. Willows and cottonwoods sometimes took root in the decaying logs of the lower raft, and dense growths of weeds and vines made it appear a solid formation. The raft could be crossed on foot—some brave souls even rode horses across it—though it was dangerous to do so. A little water passed through the raft and floods poured over the top of it, but most of the volume of the Red River was forced to flow around the Great Raft on the Texas side, creating swamps that deepened into lakes, submerging bottomlands, and forming parallel waterways. Caddo Lake was one of these marginal lakes on the eastern side of the Red River Valley, apparently forming soon after growth upstream of the Great Raft blocked the mouth of Big Cypress Bayou sometime around 1800.[3]

The period of the formation of Caddo Lake coincides with a prolonged boundary dispute over the territory of which Caddo was part, a dispute that would have long-term consequences for the human history of Wyatt Moore's special place. Disputes over boundaries; the independence, violence, and outlawry of persons attracted to a no-man's-land between governments; the great difficulty of assigning proper boundaries and jurisdictions in the confusions of a great swamp lake—these are themes that shadow Caddo down to the present and crop up again and again in Moore's narrative. Old-timers still laugh at the current U.S. Geological Survey maps, which mistakenly place the boundary between Harrison and Marion counties up Alligator Bayou to the Louisiana line, instead of in Big Cypress Channel where it should be. Swamps do not seem to be very friendly to the formal pretensions of governments, past or present. Describing a period when there had already been forty years of boundary dispute, an early account offers a glimpse of the joint Boundary Commission of the United States and the Texas Republic in its epic attempt to survey the Caddo Lake area, a vision of the State at war with the Swamp:

Owing to the peculiar formation of the northern shore, which was much cut up by inlets and swamps, considerable difficulty was

---

3. Ibid., p. 6. The raft theory of Caddo Lake's origins is also supported by historian Carl Newton Tyson in his recent work, *The Red River in Southwestern History* (Norman: University of Oklahoma Press, 1981), pp. 100–101.

experienced in marking the line on the north side of the Lake. . . .
When Jim's Bayou (also called Jeem's Bayou), one of the arms of
the Lake was reached, it was necessary to wade into the water and
cut through forests of cypress. Rafts were constructed but proved
to be of little use; the heat was excessive, the men showed great
reluctance about going into the water and the officers found it nec-
essary to take the lead.[4]

The Boundary Commission of 1841 was more or less successful in
setting the line between Texas and Louisiana, the Texas Republic and
the United States, but the basic character of the "Texas Badlands"
had been established by then. Caddo Lake would remain a place
where twentieth-century game laws were difficult to enforce, where
hunters and fishers were powerfully attached to what Moore called
"their Indian rights," where game wardens honed their skill and
speed with the .38 Special revolver (in one instance filing off the
front of a trigger guard), and where the cottage industry of moonshining was raised to a fine art.

The original boundary dispute had its origins in the inability of
the United States and Spain to agree upon a mutual boundary after
the Louisiana Purchase of 1803. In order to avert an armed clash,
General James Wilkinson and Lieutenant Colonel Simon de Herrera,
the American and Spanish military commanders respectively, on November 6, 1806, entered into an agreement declaring the disputed
territory "Neutral Ground." The boundaries of this Neutral Ground
were themselves never entirely worked out, but both sides agreed
that no settlers were to be permitted into the area. Of course, settlers
from both sides immediately rushed in. In 1819 the United States
and Spain signed the Adams-Onis Treaty purporting to define the
boundary, but this was rejected by Mexico after it won its independence from Spain. The matter was left in confusion, as before.

Meanwhile, the Neutral Zone, "No-Man's-Land," "Texas Badlands," "Texas Redlands"—it went by many names—became the
home for a considerable Anglo population, which had been self-
selected for this outlaw zone between governments. The settlers
who moved into the Texas Badlands did so in full knowledge of the
situation. They were persons who perhaps had not too much to lose,
people in search of a fresh start in a new land with little or no gov-
ernmental interference. Some were outlaws looking for a place to
reform and start over; others were outlaws simply seeking a new

---

4. Fred Tarpley, *Jefferson: Riverport to the Southwest* (Austin: Eakin Press,
1983), p. 15.

theater of operations. We are told that a customary mode of polite address in the Texas Badlands was "What was your name before you came to Texas?"

Cattle and horse rustlers and dealers in stolen slaves operated in the area as far back as 1812. Rezin and James Bowie and other persons sold contraband slaves, and there are persistent traditions that Jean Lafitte, the pirate, also frequented the Badlands. Outlaws, renegades, thieves, cutthroats, swindlers, dealers in fraudulent land certificates all came to the Badlands, for here they were outside the bounds of any nation and no law could touch them. Most of the early settlements on and around Caddo Lake were extremely rough places, but historical legends place special emphasis on the violence and villainy of Old Monterey, located near Jeems Bayou on the north side of the lake. Old Monterey became a settlement of some size, renowned for its brothels, gambling dens, rooster fights, and racetracks, as well as for a frequency of violence that set it apart even from the rest of the Texas Badlands. Moore recounts an old historical legend about an impromptu duel between two residents of the area. One man fires a pistol at close range while the other flings a heavy pair of blacksmith tongs, with mutually fatal results. Old Monterey was one of those frontier settlements known as "the place where they kill a man every day."[5]

Some of the residents of the Texas Badlands, perhaps most of them, did not register their land in either the United States or Texas. Others, more cautious, registered in both places. The government of the Texas Republic was well aware of the brisk trade moving through the settlements in and around Caddo Lake, and, in the case of Port Caddo on the south shore of the lake, made a considerable effort to collect taxes and customs from an area it regarded as part of its national domain. This proved very difficult. Accustomed to being left alone without benefit of government, courts, or other public services, the natives of Port Caddo resisted these attempts. One would-be tax collector was murdered in broad daylight on the streets of Port Caddo and his tax records burned on the spot. Attempts to set up a customs office were no more successful, as the customs officer and his three helpers were run out of town under threat of death.[6]

The period of the Texas Republic also witnessed the greatest outbreak of violence in the history of the Texas Badlands in the form of

---

5. Mildred Mays McClung, "Caddo Lake—Moss-Draped Swampland of Mystery" (Thesis, East Texas State University, 1955), pp. 54–55.

6. V. H. Hackney, *Port Caddo—A Vanished Village and Vignettes of Harrison County* (Marshall, Tex.: Marshall National Bank, 1966), p. 16.

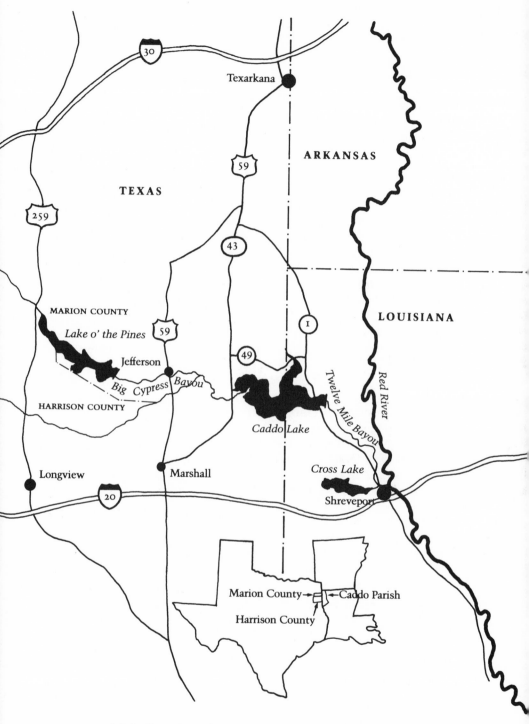

MAP 1. *Ark-La-Tex region. After a map by James H. Conrad.*

the "Regulator-Moderator War." The trouble grew directly from the general lawlessness of the place and the uncertainty of land claims in the Neutral Ground. Only the beginnings are very clear. The feud started when Charles W. Jackson killed Joseph G. Goodbread in Shelbyville after a quarrel over forged land certificates. Jackson was tried and acquitted by a "managed" court and promptly organized a band of men he called "Regulators," avowedly to suppress crime. They launched upon a career of vigilante justice which included beatings, arson, and murder, and their perceived excesses stimulated the formation of an opposing vigilante group, the "Moderators," who got their name from an intent to moderate the actions of the Regulators. Charles W. Jackson was waylaid and killed by these Moderators, and at this point the battle really was joined.[7]

Only the outlines of what took place between 1839 and 1844 are recorded, but it is obvious that the area was in the throes of near civil war. The mass of citizens, who would probably have preferred to remain neutral, were forced to choose sides. There were major pitched battles between scores—sometimes hundreds—of combatants. There are accounts of assassins hired in Austin to go to Shelby County and kill seventeen men, of killings in the Harrison County city hall, courthouse, hotels, and streets—even in community dances and at church. Perhaps the most famous casualty of the violence was Robert Potter, the former Secretary of the Texas Navy. Potter and his wife, Harriet, had settled at Potter's Point on the north shore of the lake. Potter, a Moderator, became embroiled in a bitter personal feud with another local landowner, Captain Pinkey Rose, a leader of the local Regulators. Potter and his supporters unsuccessfully attempted to capture Rose, who soon reciprocated with a deadly attack of his own. Awakening to a house surrounded by Rose's men, and disregarding his wife's pleas to stay inside to fight it out, Potter ran for the lake. Dropping his gun at the edge, he swam for safety underwater, but when his head broke the surface Rose's Regulators shot him dead.

Less-known or forgotten conflicts similar to the Rose-Potter feud went on everywhere. The feud split communities, neighborhoods, and families. As the violence went on with no end in sight, some people built defensive fortifications of impressive size. Colonel Boulware, a Regulator leader, had so many enemies that he was afraid to leave his home after dark. He built a huge blockhouse, a fort made of immense logs with firing slots for rifles and heavily timbered doors. Boulware told a visiting clergyman who came to Mar-

7. R. B. Blake, "Regulator-Moderator War," *Handbook of Texas*, vol. 2 (Austin: Texas State Historical Association, 1952), p. 458.

shall and spent a night in the famous blockhouse something that many other residents of the Texas Badlands must have felt: "No money on earth could ever again tempt me to live where the law is incapable of affording protection to life and property."[8]

The Regulator-Moderator feud finally came to an end in 1844 after Texas President Sam Houston made an impassioned patriotic plea to both sides to lay down their arms and at the same time sent in five-hundred outside militia. One or the other worked; like Colonel Boulware, most people probably were heartily tired of living in an outlaw zone after five long years of violence and social disorder.

But bad blood—and personal feuds—festered in the area for decades, merging into another time of troubles that came after the Civil War. Reconstruction was particularly violent and bitter in the former Texas Badlands. Working in the 1950's, historian Mildred McClung recorded a large body of folklore and oral traditional history about the decades just after the Civil War in the Caddo Lake area.[9] Any individual account might be in question, but the general historical message was clear; once again the area had been the scene of outlawry and social disorder, as the traditional Badlands distaste for authority was intensified by the presence of a "foreign" army of occupation from the North.

McClung recorded a whole complex of stories about one man, Cullen Baker, a sort of local "Jesse James." These were "tales . . . learned in conversation with men who heard them from their parents." Baker terrorized and murdered freed slaves and Yankees during the late 1860's and early 1870's, aided and abetted (or so the stories go) by unreconstructed rebels and rebel sympathizers, and he may have killed as many as fifty men. In any case, he is clearly one of those violence-prone Robin Hoods that the folk memory likes to work over and make into something very different, perhaps, from what they really were. One hundred-year-old eyewitness described Baker as a man of slight stature, weighing about 140 pounds, who always carried a big, double-barreled shotgun and rode a "pacing mule" named Nell. It is said that at the time of his death Baker carried his usual shotgun, four six-shooters, three derringers, and twenty-seven keys of various kinds. Betrayed by supposed friends and killed in his sleep, he is one of those historical ghosts of the place that until quite recently persisted in living memory. Once again, it is a violent ghost.

8. McClung, "Caddo Lake," p. 66.
9. Ibid., pp. 76–87.

Wyatt Moore is not himself a violent man (though he does admit to a fistfight or two), but the old-timers he fished and hunted with in his youth were survivors from the Cullen Baker era, the bloody days of Reconstruction. Their speech and stories were full of the echoes of that earlier time. Extreme independence and a related propensity for violence are two of the major historical themes of the place, and crop up in the actions of others at many places in Moore's otherwise peaceful narrative about getting a living on and around Caddo Lake. The old cultural traditions of the Texas Badlands were hard to leave completely behind, and persisted in notions of "Indian rights" and game wardens who felt it necessary to practice their pistol skills. Moore has a clipping which reports that in one year in the 1950's more illegal stills were found and destroyed in Harrison County than in all the other Texas counties combined.

When Wyatt Moore was growing up in the years before World War I, Cullen Baker and his kind were present only in the memories of the old, but the real historical ghosts that haunt Caddo Lake were still there to be seen. These were the decaying hulks of the great steamboats, killed by long-lost disasters and still protruding above the waters of the lake, mute reminders of Caddo's golden age of steam and commerce.

Just as Caddo Lake was a by-product of the Great Raft on the Red River, so was its age of steamboats. The raft diverted such vast quantities of water from the main channel of the Red into the Sodo-Caddo chain of lakes that steamboat travel was possible seven or eight months out of the year, depending on the amount of rainfall and the level of the lake. After leaving Shreveport, the boats used several routes to enter Caddo, the choice of which depended upon the existing water level. One route was by way of Cross Bayou and Cross Lake, then the Sodo Lake chain to Caddo. Another route went up Twelve Mile Bayou, through Sodo, thence into Caddo Lake. At the entrance to Caddo the steamboats had to pick their way across a shallow stretch called Albany Flats, which was a result of the settling out of silt from the waters of the Red River when they entered the lake. Here, there were several channels that were constantly changing as the river shifted the sediments around.

Steamboat captains began to find their way around the western side of the Great Raft and into Caddo Lake in the 1830's, thus bringing a new era of commerce and economic development. The first ports of call on the lake were Potter's Point on the north and Wray's Bluff on the south. When Americans poured into the area after Texas Independence, others were quickly established, including Port Caddo,

Tuscumbia, Smithland, Swanson's Landing, Williams Bluff (Old Monterey), Baldwin, and Clinton. It should be noted that these were major ports of call, not simple landings; landings at private plantations and woodyards were much more numerous.

Until the mid-1840's Caddo Lake was regarded as the head of navigation, and Big Cypress Bayou was rarely tried. Gradually, Port Caddo and Swanson's Landing, both on the south shore of the lake, became the main ports of call, only to be themselves eclipsed by the rise of Jefferson in the 1850's. A steamboat reached Jefferson in 1845 with 130 passengers aboard, and soon the settlement was firmly established as the head of navigation for Caddo Lake, being thirty torturous river miles from the first open water of the lake. The heyday of Jefferson and the golden age of Caddo Lake were thus begun.

As Fred Tarpley notes in his history of Jefferson, by 1849 steamboats were running on regular schedules and the community had become a flourishing commercial center of sixty houses, stores, a warehouse, a gristmill, and a small sawmill.[10] This frontier outpost was now linked to the riverine civilization of New Orleans by only five days' travel, and the look of Jefferson, a crude log settlement a decade before, was swiftly transformed. The architecture of Jefferson's homes quickly began to resemble the Greek Revival styles of the Garden District of New Orleans, and the latest fashions in clothing, delicacies in food, and architectural designs were suddenly available to prosperous Jeffersonians as steamboat cargoes.

Traffic to Jefferson increased during the 1850's, and by 1860 the port was by far the largest trading center in North Texas, and second only to Galveston as a Texas shipping point. Cotton, wheat, hides, lumber—all the products of a region as large as many states of the Union—made their way to Jefferson to be loaded on the steamboats. Historian Eugene C. Barker estimates that at one time one-fourth of the entire trade of Texas passed through Jefferson.[11] On the return trip, the steamers that threaded the twisting channel of Big Cypress Bayou brought to Jefferson the manufactured goods of other sections of the United States and of foreign lands, which were then distributed westward by wagon to Sherman, Dallas, Fort Worth, and other outlying settlements. The wagon trade to the west was so large that roads were often jammed for miles. In 1860, Jefferson had a cotton export trade of 100,000 bales—second only to Galveston's 148,000 bales.[12]

---

10. Tarpley, *Jefferson*, p. 52.
11. Quoted by McClung, "Caddo Lake," p. 37.
12. Ibid.

The role played by Jefferson during the Civil War only increased its size and prominence. Ninety miles away from the nearest military engagement (the battle of Mansfield, Louisiana), Jefferson served as one of the leading supply depots for the Confederate Army in the Trans-Mississippi Department.

Jefferson's boom continued through the mid-1870's, at which time the population of the city peaked somewhere around eight-thousand. The town was a bustling commercial center, featuring such technological wonders as a system of downtown lighting utilizing pine-knot gas and one of the earliest ice-making machines in the United States. During this period Jefferson played host to many important personages, including a variety of steamboat tycoons, Presidents Grant and Hayes, Oscar Wilde, John Jacob Astor, and W. H. Vanderbilt.

Like the cotton that went out and the fine trappings of New Orleans civilization that came in, all these persons rode to and from Jefferson upon the broad backs of the great steamboats. For half a century the captains picked their ways across Albany Flats into Caddo Lake, thence to every settlement and landing on lake and river. They were chancy, romantic things, these steamboats. Caddo historian Fred Dahmer has made a study of them, and his description is well worth quoting. Henry Miller Shreve is credited with inventing the "western river steamboat," and despite the fact that the first trial of his new design resulted in an explosion killing thirteen men, the boat, which used very high pressure steam, caught on.

Shreve's design used a shallow raft-like body, with boiler and high pressure horizontal engine on the main deck, a stern paddle wheel connected by a crank to the engine, and a deck above the main deck for a wheelhouse. The design was well adapted to the western rivers with their shallow waters and swift currents; but it was also a very dangerous one, and ushered in an era of terrible disasters in river transportation. The boilers on the main deck were among and close to their own fuel, the ship's cargo, which often consisted of highly inflammable cotton, tallow, hay, etc., and the passengers. The boiler operated at higher pressures than was safe for the stage of development and metallurgy of the time. Also, the wide, flat-bottomed, low-sided hull, built entirely of wood, was inherently very weak (compared to a regular ship's hull) and required rope and cable trusses and guys to stiffen it. To put it bluntly; if the boat didn't catch afire, and the boiler didn't blow up, it probably sank when it hit a snag![13]

13. Fred Dahmer, "Caddo Was," Ch. 3, *Greater Caddo Lake Association News* 4 (October 1980): 2.

These steamboats were simple enough to be built in small boatyards without elaborate facilities, but they soon evolved into floating palaces of great luxury. Today, it is difficult to stand on the bridge over Big Cypress Bayou at Jefferson, looking down at the narrow stream, and envision the presence of the *Era No. 11*, 245 feet long, capable of carrying 4,500 bales of cotton and 700 head of cattle. Yet this boat regularly reached Jefferson. The steamboats were classified as "1,000-bale boats," "2,000-bale boats," and so forth, so the *Era No. 11* was a 4,500-bale boat and one of the largest that ever came up the river. Most steamboats were from 150 to 200 feet long, but many drew as little as 12 inches of water before loading. They were specialized, shallow-draft stern-wheelers. The stern wheels allowed them to be narrow—sometimes exactly as narrow as Big Cypress Bayou at its most constricted point. The tall smokestacks were hinged so that they could be lowered by pulley to lie on top of the pilot's cabin in order to pass under overhanging limbs.

Some were the disorderly tramp steamers of their day. Such a boat was described by an irate former passenger around 1840 in wonderfully evocative terms. The vessel, according to the passenger,

should be named Discord *[rather than* Concord*], for the fireman abused the mate, the cook fought the steward, the mosquitoes waged war on the passengers, and the passengers are not yet done cursing mate, fireman, steward, mosquitoes—in fine, the boat and all connected with her. A more miserable, dirty, slow moving, improvised, chicken thievish craft never walked the waters. . . . it excites my spleen to think of her.*[14]

If the much-abused *Concord* represented one extreme, the flagship 200-footers represented the other. Top-of-the-line steamboats vied with each other to attain the greatest opulence, the greatest luxury, the best Italian band, the most complicated menu. The passengers' cabin, sometimes 200 feet long, was a "long resplendent tunnel" separating staterooms and serving as social hall and dining room. Elaborately carved brackets supported high ceilings decorated with gothic ornaments. The light from stained glass windows fell on many-colored Brussels carpets, imported chandeliers, paintings, rich draperies, ornate furniture, and grand pianos, all reflected in towering mirrors at the end of the cabin. The steamers all had their own special silverware, china, linens, fine dining tables, and the like. Here is a selection from one ship's menu documenting what was served aboard the *R. H. Powell* on March 27, 1845:

---

14. Quoted by Tarpley, *Jefferson*, p. 50.

*Entres: geletin poulard, allspice jelly, magalenes of whiting a la
Venetienne; patted-chaud of godveiau a la ciboulette; breast of
mutton, braised with green peas; geletin turkey, with allspice
jelly; stuffed shoulder of mutton, garnished with oysters; tender-
loin steak with French fried potatoes; gelatin hogshead, allspice
jelly; hogshead a la Florentine; stuffed crabs and oyster pie; roast
beef, mutton, veal, pork, pig.*[15]

And then, of course, there was a modest dessert including such things
as "currant, apple, cranberry and cherry pie; pound, jelly, sponge
and fruit cakes . . . vanilla and lemon custards, ice cream, cream
cakes," etc.

When the steamboat docked at a plantation landing or settlement
on the way into Jefferson, the passengers dressed elaborately in
clothes carried in enormous trunks and prepared to dance the waltz
or schottische at fancy balls, which were often held outside under
hundreds of lanterns. Steamboats had their own Italian bands that
played on such occasions, at dinners on board, and at other times. On
the decks of the steamers, Negro roustabouts worked eighteen-hour
days singing and keeping time with their feet to a very different form
of music, the strange, haunting songs known as "Coonjines," which
until recently could still be heard around Caddo Lake. Cargoes were
efficiently distributed by the illiterate deckhands on the basis of an
ingenious playing-card marker system, goods for Jefferson being des-
ignated by the "King of Spades," Longview by the "Ace of Hearts,"
Marshall by the "King of Hearts," etc.

Resplendent and luxurious though they may have been, the steamboats were still dangerous. Dahmer writes:

*The resinous heartwood found in the stumps, roots and cores of
pine trees was called "fat wood," and was burned in a basket on
the wheelhouse with a reflector behind it, to light the way when
the boat traveled by night. Can you imagine a dark and windy
night with a steamer, boiler fireboxes flaring open on the main
deck, "searchlight" streaming flames and embers above the wheelhouse; all amidst a cargo of hay, cotton, gunpowder, etc. on the
same deck with the fuel and "fat wood," slowly picking its way
through Broad Lake?*[16]

This was the situation aboard the *Mittie Stephens* on the night of
February 11, 1869. The 312-ton steamboat had left Shreveport at

15. Ibid., p. 56.
16. Fred Dahmer, "Caddo Was," Ch. 4, *Greater Caddo Lake Association
News* 5 (December 1980): 2.

4 P.M. carrying over one-hundred passengers. Sometime around midnight the *Mittie's* luck ran out, as hay on the deck caught fire in a stiff wind. The boat immediately made for shore and grounded at the bow within a few minutes. Unfortunately, by that time the fire at the front end of the boat was so intense that no one could get by it. Passengers were forced to abandon ship at the stern, 160 feet offshore in the frigid lake. A Mr. Lodwick, one of the *Mittie's* steersmen, gave a vivid report of the tragedy to *The Caddo Gazette* in Shreveport. Lodwick described the panic, that, along with the fire, the still-churning paddle wheel, and the cold water, took the life of sixty of the *Mittie Stephens'* passengers.

Everything was thrown overboard that could be made available to save life. The yawl was overloaded, and we are told the terror-stricken occupants remained in it until the tow-line was burned in two when all sank together. The scene is represented by the survivors to have been horrible beyond expression. A hundred human beings, men, women and children frantic with terror, a fiery death behind and a watery grave before them—dread alternative, indeed! Husbands and wives, parents and children were madly calling to each other, and poor helpless women frantically shrieking for help where no help could come.

As the flames advanced the men leaped overboard and there was for a time a sea of heads above the water. The heart sickens at the thought of the scenes that ensued—men fighting madly for something to cling to and sinking in this death struggle to rise no more. . . . Doubtless, many expert swimmers were drawn under by others clinging to them with the grasp of despair, and, too, the waves caused by the wheels of the boat, as the engines had not been stopped, materially impeded escape.[17]

Within less than one hour after the fire had first broken out, the steamboat was a charred hulk.

Wyatt Moore's mother once owned a washpan that had come from the *Mittie Stephens,* and other metallic bits and pieces of the *Mittie's* gear lingered for years in the hands of people who lived in and around Swanson's Landing. The steamboat trade itself would survive the death of the *Mittie Stephens* by only a decade or so. Efforts to clear the Great Raft on the Red River had begun as early as 1833, but it was 1873 before the raft was finally cleared and sufficient funds allocated to keep it that way. Shreveport had long been jealous of the

17. Quoted by Tarpley, *Jefferson,* p. 119.

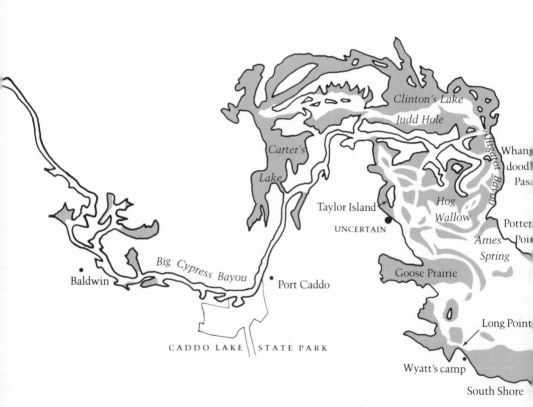

MAP 2. *Caddo Lake. After a map by James H. Conrad.*

SMITHLAND

Clinton's Lake

Judd Hole

Carter's

Lake

Alligator Bayou

Whang

dood

Pas

Taylor Island

Hog

Wallow

UNCERTAIN

Potter

Poi

Ames

Spring

Big Cypress Bayou

Baldwin

Port Caddo

Goose Prairie

Long Point

CADDO LAKE STATE PARK

Wyatt's camp

South Shore

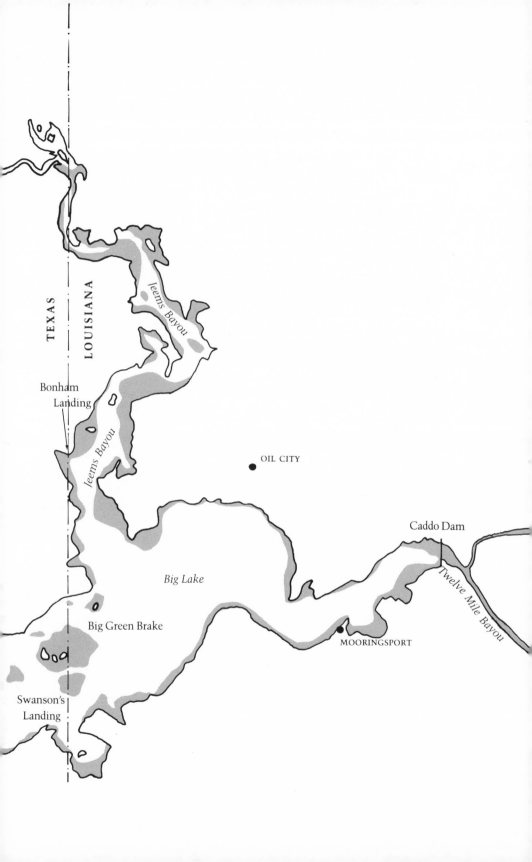

prosperity of Jefferson, longing to play its natural role as premier river port on the Red River, and was a persistent lobbyist to the U.S. government for removal of the raft. After 1873 this was done, and from Shreveport's perspective two birds were killed with a single stone. The route up the Red River at last was cleared for steamboat traffic and economic development, while the plug was pulled on Caddo Lake and Jefferson, Texas. Gradually at first, month by month and year by year, the marginal lakes on the Texas side of the Red River Valley began to drain. Such was the size of Caddo, and the great extent of sediments now blocking it off from the river, that its drainage was only partial. The water level fell only a very few feet, but that was enough. The trip up the lake to Jefferson had always been a difficult run. Now, for long months of the year, it was impossible. Caddo Lake's steamboat era dwindled to a close. The sound of ship's bell and steam whistle, the sight of the great boats majestically walking up the lake in daylight or carefully picking their way by night, fat pine searchlights blazing, became a thing of memory. Finally, only the dead hulks of steamboats remained, resting on the shallow lake bottom.

Moore remembers the derelicts. Like Caddo Lake itself, he has been to a degree haunted by these ghosts of the place. He has read about steamboats, visited steamboat museums on the Mississippi, and interviewed his mother at length about her memories of steamboat days. Although it was not a stern-wheeler, one of Moore's restorations of the large cypress motor launches of master boatbuilder Frank Galbraith was renamed *The African Queen*. Moore once invited Katharine Hepburn to come down for a day's steam about the lake, but the actress did not reply. Moore and an artist friend, Don Brown from Shreveport, piloted what was perhaps the last sternwheeler to run on Caddo Lake, a 35-footer powered by a Model A engine.

The end of steamboat commerce had drastic effects on the Caddo Lake culture and economy. Jefferson reverted to its earlier backwater status, dying on the twisting vine of Big Cypress Bayou. The era of steamboats, Greek Revival homes, and "magalenes of whiting a la Venetienne" devolved into a time of "pullin' skiffs," board-and-batten cabins, and catfish and beans, as the natives of Caddo were thrown back on the resources of the lake. The link with the money economy of New Orleans was gone, and Caddo was once again a backwater, but a rich backwater. Fred Dahmer aptly describes the situation:

*There was little chance of not eating well, for Caddo provided an
abundance of fish, wildfowl, squirrel, rabbit, deer and all sorts of
wild game. Chinquapins, black walnuts, hickory nuts, persim-
mons, muscadines and wild grapes were harvested in the Fall.
Mayhaws, blackberries, dewberries, wild plums, Indian peaches
and all sorts of things began to ripen in early Summer. . . . Our
Caddo Lake folks lived quite well—yet, they did require a little
cash money occasionally for such things as flour, salt, nails, shot,
gunpowder, fish hooks, twine, etc. So, they turned to commercial
hunting and fishing. The commercial fishes were usually buffalo
and catfish. The commercial game was generally ducks, geese,
deer, squirrel and rabbit. All were easy to get and salable, and the
supply seemed unending. The paddlefish, known locally as "spoonbill catfish," were netted for their roe, which was shipped to eastern markets and there sold as "caviar" at a premium price. . . .
[Later] hundreds, perhaps thousands, of people joined in the search
for freshwater pearls in Caddo Lake.*[18]

Wyatt Moore's life has been spent in this post-steamboat era of
hunting, fishing, timbering, and small-farming, and like many natives of the place he often has had to work at several things at one
time to get by. Money was often hard to find, but the rich resources
of the lake were always there to fall back on. Trapped in the house
he built on the north side of the lake by a great snowstorm in the
1930's, Moore had no stock of food to feed his wife and two daughters, but had only to walk a few yards down to the lake, chop a hole
in the ice, and catch a meal of white perch. It was hard to get rich on
Caddo Lake, but it was also hard to starve.

Moonshining was one source of ready cash that Fred Dahmer does
not mention, and Moore became a canny master of the art and sci-
ence of liquor distillation in primitive circumstances. Moore understood, along with a great many of his neighbors, that swamps, besides being rich sources of fish, fowl, and game, were also wonderful
places to hide things. In his narrative that follows, we are offered a
rare glimpse of the master moonshiner at work, un-apprehended and
unrepentant. Moore is neither particularly proud nor particularly
ashamed of his moonshining and illicit fishing and hunting activities. Most of his neighbors did these things too, though perhaps with
less success. These were just some of the things folks in a money-
poor economy had to do after the steamboats were gone.

---

18. Fred Dahmer, "Caddo Was," Ch. 6, *Greater Caddo Lake Association
News* 7 (April 1981): 2.

Wyatt Moore has approached all the occupations of his long life with an uncommon energy and audacity. He is a self-taught mechanical wizard, a lifelong "projector," as he terms it. Others raised hogs and churned milk; Moore designed air-conditioned hogpens and electric churns. Most moonshiners were content with a single method of aging their product; Moore tried many different methods, including one which utilized the services of the U.S. Mail Boat on Caddo Lake. Although the reader will find no account of Moore's water-well rigs in the following narrative (for once, language entirely broke down as a means of description!), he has constructed fully functional water-well drilling outfits from the rear ends of dead trucks and mechanical bits and pieces from the oil fields. In later life, Moore has specialized in mechanical miracles which raised from the dead several of the expensive motor launches originally built for rich oilmen by his friend Frank Galbraith. Like the proverbial Indian who takes the white man's "dead" horse up from the ground and rides it fifty miles, Moore lifted from the mud the boats he renamed *Tush Hog* and *African Queen* and used them to probe the sloughs and channels of Caddo Lake for decades.

And always, whatever his occupations of the moment, Moore has observed and explored his native place, Caddo Lake, with an inexhaustible fascination. For most of us, the locale we are born in and grow up in literally becomes invisible, an unexamined given, part of the general background. Not so for Moore. Throughout his life he has sought out the artifacts, the documents, the living memories that had something to tell him about Caddo Lake, and has learned from them all. In some curious way he has come to embody as much as one human mind can the whole experience of the place—a rich legacy of steamboats and swamp, of deeds done and memories of men and women long dead.

The oral life history of Wyatt A. Moore is the first product of the Caddo Lake Oral History Project of East Texas State University. The project seeks to record the environmental oral history of Caddo Lake and environs. The focus of the project is upon "man-land" interactions at Caddo—the many occupations and avocations that tie human beings to the physical environments in which they live and die. At Caddo Lake the project is recording oral accounts of timbering, fishing, hunting, and moonshining, as well as such exotics as the early pearling industry and the offshore oil drilling in the lake during the first decades of this century. This is an enterprise in cultural geography, folklore, cultural anthropology, or social history, depending on one's point of view. The definitions and theoretical approaches may differ, but the material is the same.

That Moore's story should be the first publication seems entirely appropriate, since the project itself began with Moore. In 1981 Thad Sitton was leafing through *The Texas Sampler*, a Bicentennial publication of the Governor's Commission on Aging published in 1976, when he discovered a chapter featuring Wyatt Moore entitled "Wild Things in Caddo Lake." The usual approach of the *Sampler's* editors (Donna Bearden and Jamie Frucht) was to interview elderly persons to record their interesting life experiences, then present this material in a more or less standard journalistic manner. Only with Moore did they depart from the pattern. Moore's chapter was printed verbatim, told entirely in his own words, and from this colorful and detailed account of outlaw fishing, moonshining, and other "wild things," it became perfectly clear that here was a man with a unique story to tell and a great power to tell it. The question was, after a lapse of over five years was Wyatt Moore still alive, well, and willing to talk? A phone call to Karnack, Texas, answered all three questions in the emphatic affirmative. In response to his would-be oral historians Moore said, in effect, "What kept you?"

Wyatt Moore's story suggested the idea of an environmentally focused oral history of Caddo Lake, and our first order of business was to completely debrief the star interviewee. This took some time! In the process, we discovered not only that others had gone before us in interviewing Wyatt but also that they were generously willing to allow their interview material to be incorporated with our own. Several years before, Moore had collaborated with an old friend, Judge Franklin Jones, Sr., of Marshall, to record several hours of taped remembrances. These tapes were a virtual self-interview, with Jones the interviewer offering only an occasional prod as Moore told his story from childhood to the present. These earlier tapes became the narrative framework upon which all the rest of the interview material would be hung.

Another extensive series of tapes had been recorded by Moore's close friends Paul Ray and Anna Martin of Uncertain, Texas. The Martins have a lake house on Taylor Island near Karnack, and Moore was a frequent visitor in their home. He and they gradually evolved a pattern of recording his anecdotal accounts on the Martins' tape recorder as these were remembered. When a new incident or personal story occurred to Wyatt, the recorder would be turned on, then set aside to await the arrival of the next remembrance. Gradually, over a year or so, a rich store of vintage Moore was accumulated on a number of tapes and filed away in a desk drawer. The Martins' tapes were informal, colorful, and anecdotal in nature, focused on many specific events and individuals, and—like Moore himself in casual circumstances—often of a humorous turn.

Finally, we ourselves conducted several hours of interviews with Wyatt Moore, eliciting much greater detail on the key topics of commercial fishing, hunting, boatbuilding, oil-field work, moonshining, and other aspects of the natural and occupational history of the Caddo Lake area. Portions of these tapes were like the long soliloquies of Franklin Jones' recordings (Wyatt seems quite comfortable with the soliloquy!), but other parts resembled the back-and-forth pattern of normal conversation.

In the end, the narrative framework of Jones was fleshed out with the detail of Sitton and Conrad and the anecdotes and stories recorded by the Martins to produce this book. As editors, we took certain necessary liberties in moving Moore's words around, very few with the words themselves. Everything seemed to fit into place. As Helena Huntington Smith said of memoirist "Teddy Blue" Abbott, "In his rush and drive to tell his story it came out helter-skelter, all over place and time. . . . But afterwards, when I fitted the pieces together, they dovetailed with never a hairbreadth inconsistency in dates and facts."[19]

This book has finally come to be a much more detailed and elaborated version of the sequence of topics explored in Moore's long, impromptu narrative taped for Franklin Jones several years ago. The editors have done their proper job, but in the end *Every Sun That Rises* is all Moore's. It could hardly be otherwise, given the force of the man's personality. He has read every word, corrected spellings of personal and place names, and otherwise pronounced it a true account. As Smith said of her "Teddy Blue," "He has been carving this book inside himself for years. . . . My [our] part was to keep out of the way and not mess it up by being literary."[20]

The Caddo Lake Oral History Project is grateful to several persons who have helped to record and edit Wyatt Moore's telling of his own story. We owe a great debt of gratitude to Paul Ray and Anna Martin of Taylor Island, who have made their home the project's informal base of operations at Caddo Lake, and whose many recordings of Wyatt added immeasurably to the richness of the finished product. Without Paul's able assistance to Moore, the bateau-building experiment could never have succeeded. Our thanks also for the recordings

19. E. C. Abbott ("Teddy Blue") and Helena Huntington Smith, *We Pointed Them North: Recollections of a Cowpuncher* (Norman: University of Oklahoma Press, 1939), p. vi.

20. Ibid., p. viii.

of Wyatt made by Franklin Jones, Sr., of Marshall. These tapes made by Moore's good friends, old and new, made possible a much more detailed, colorful, and intimate story than would otherwise have been told. Thanks also to historians Fred Tarpley of East Texas State University and Fred Dahmer of Uncertain, Texas, for their advice and assistance. Finally, we are especially grateful to the Texas Committee for the Humanities for its grant supporting the construction of Wyatt Moore's "Last Caddo Bateau."

THAD SITTON AND JAMES H. CONRAD

Chronological Notes

Wyatt A. Moore was born the first child of William Henry ("Black Bill") Moore and Lizzie Hannah Bonner Moore on October 2, 1901, at Karnack, Texas. The family lived on a hundred-acre farm inherited from William Moore's father about one-half mile from town. Wyatt's brothers were Henry, Jr., Vernon Hatley, and Walter Lewis. His one sister, Mary Naomi, died at sixteen.

Wyatt attended the one-room Karnack School through the ninth grade. He worked on the family farm and at about age fourteen went to work on timber rafts bringing cypress pilings to oil field operations on the eastern end of Caddo Lake. In 1916–1917 he worked with his uncle at a commercial fishing camp on Big Lake. Later in 1917 he went for the first time to the Louisiana oil fields, working as a roustabout and living with an aunt and uncle. Most of Wyatt's family followed him to the oil fields in 1918, staying for the better part of a year before returning to Karnack. Sometime in late 1918 or early 1919 Wyatt returned to Caddo Lake and his uncle's fishing camp, then relocated to Baldwin on Big Cypress Bayou to run a store in partnership with the same uncle. For the next few years Wyatt continued to fish with his uncle and brother, began to make whiskey, and worked intermittently in the oil fields.

In 1925 Wyatt married Ona Belle Hayner and went to the oil fields near Waskom, Louisiana. Between 1925 and 1929 he worked in the oil fields; worked as a hatchery man for the Game, Fish and Oyster Commission at Tyler, Dallas, and Cisco, Texas; and worked in the Texas Pacific Railroad shops at Marshall.

In 1929 Wyatt built a lake camp at Long Point (now called Big Lake Camp) on the south shore of Caddo Lake. Wyatt did a little bit of everything during his next fourteen years (1929–1943) at his lake camp, a period he refers to as the most satisfying part of his life. He was a camp operator, commercial fisherman, commercial hunter, boatbuilder, water-well driller, farmer, boat operator and repairman, and professional moonshiner. During this period Wyatt's two daughters were born, Gloria in 1931 and Martha in 1933, the latter birth coinciding with the all-time high-water mark at Caddo Lake.

In 1943 he left the lake camp, moved his family to a house at the site of his present home at Karnack, and went to work for a new war industry, the Longhorn Ordnance Plant. His jobs there over the next twenty-three years included security and contractor work. After his retirement at age sixty-five in 1966 he still worked occasionally for the plant. He worked as guide for Walt Disney Productions during one of their movies filmed at Caddo Lake. After restoration of *The Tush Hog*, a cypress motor launch built years before by Moore's friend Frank Galbraith, Wyatt was employed as boatman by the Corps of Engineers in a snag-clearing operation on Big Cypress Bayou in 1973, and in 1975 he used *The Tush Hog* to help drive pilings for Southwest Electric Power Company. Since 1978 he has, as he says, fished, hunted, worked as pipeline watchman, and "done a little bit of everything."

Wyatt Moore

Wyatt Moore

Everything I have is wore out, broke down, falling over, or rotting off. I wouldn't have anything new. Even if I did, I wouldn't show it to you.

It's terrible when you know so much to do and ain't able to do it. There was an old man in Marshall, done got feeble and setting in the house, Deke's wife's dad. I can't think of his name. Several years ago he was there and I would visit with him. Me and Bill Wadlington had chased hogs down here in the military reservation and caught some, and finally built a pen down there, and caught thirty some-odd and put 'em in a boat and brought 'em home and eat some of 'em and sold 'em and fooled around with 'em. We was telling this old man about it and he said, "God dog Moore, ain't it hell to be in the shape I'm in and can't get out and have sport like that!" He called it sport chasing them wild hogs through the woods. I'm beginning to remember what he said now.

And there was another old man at Karnack, Uncle George Redden, the same age as my dad, born the same day. He lived down there with his son-in-law Tommy Lamb a good many years after my dad died. Billy Jenkins, my old friend, lived over there a ways across from Uncle George, and on a cool morning Uncle George would set out beside the house in a straight chair leaned back there in the sunshine and kind of get warmed up. One day Uncle Billy was walking over towards there, and Uncle George was setting there with his mouth open and head leaning over. He'd raise up, then go back to sleep and his head would drop. But then he saw Uncle Billy and spoke up. He had a good heavy voice, says, "Uncle Billy!" Says, "Yessah, Uncle George, what is it?" Says, "Do you get to feel ah many dese young girls anymore?" Billy says, "Well, naw, not much, Uncle George. Sometimes though. How come you ask?" George says, "I jus wonduh, do de feel like de use to?"

I don't know what Billy answered, but I believe they do. I was born in the year one, you know—nineteen-hundred-and-one—that's been a far piece ago, down there at Karnack. That was about the time the railroad came, the time T. J. Taylor, Lady Bird Johnson's daddy, came. The steamboats had quit coming just a few years before that, so I heard lots of steamboat talk.

They were sixty to seventy feet long, maybe twenty feet wide or so, kind of flat-bottomed and come to a point on the front. Like the *Delta Queen* and the ones you see on the Mississippi, only on a smaller scale. They were stern-wheelers and side-wheelers. Seems that I recall that the side-wheelers were more common in the early days. The old *Sprague* down there at Vicksburg, which is still afloat in its museum, is an enormous thing and a side-wheeler. The wheels are forty feet big, and when they made those revolutions, it would walk 120 feet. They didn't turn 'em very fast. The bigger the wheel, the slower you're turning, because the outer edge of it is traveling faster. The purpose is to build the wheel big and turn it slow. Then, when it's walking, several of the blades are down in the water at once. If you build a little wheel and put in on the back of the boat, it defeats your purpose, because a lot of your energy is pushing down and lifting the boat. Then it's just lifting the water as it comes up behind it. It's just not a forward propulsion. The bigger the wheel, the more economical you were.

The paddle wheel didn't stick in the water very deep. It had boards on it you could replace if they got broke. They weren't so wide, but the idea was to have the wheel big enough where three or four of the paddles were in the water at once. If you don't, if you don't build the wheel right, it'll jump or bounce. They'll be a slack place, and it will run a little fast until the next one gets there, then it'll pound like. I fiddle with paddle wheels a little.

The steamboats run from Red River through to Caddo Lake, then up Big Cypress River to Jefferson. My mother [Lizzie Bonner Moore] was only eight or nine years old when they quit running. She was born in 1889, which means that they quit running pretty quick after that. Other big landings on the lake besides Swanson's were Smith's Landing, Port Caddo, Bonham Landing, Stacy Landing, and probably some landing at Uncertain. The *Mittie Stephens* apparently was coming upstream and sank before it got to Swanson's Landing in the night. It had a load of hay on up front, and it caught fire from some torches they had lighted. Somebody on the boat didn't want to run at night, but some of the zealous crew wanted to proceed on, and improvised torches, and caught it on fire and destroyed themselves. The story is that the fire occurred on the front of the boat, which means that the engine and paddle wheel were about amidships and it was a side-wheeler. The crew turned it into shore and rammed it up against the shore and jumped off, maybe through the fire before it got too bad. For the passengers in the back, the fire had become so intense they couldn't get off the boat. Some of 'em jumped out in the river attempting to escape and get around to the bank, but the paddle wheels were left turning and the current from them pushed them out in the lake and they drowned. Might have been partly burned, I don't know.

Back when the *Mittie Stephens* sank, the lake was probably three or four feet higher than it is now. There is quite a move here to try to locate and pick up and restore and put in a museum the old *Mittie Stephens*. Well, they don't know that the *Mittie Stephens* sank out on what is now dry land. My grandmother [Mary Alabama Cooley Moore] told me some things about the *Mittie Stephens*. They salvaged some of the things off it—I can remember she mentioned a washpot—and hid them until the investigation was over. My uncle used to point out about where they understood it was, about a mile downstream from Swanson's Landing. The Texas A&M people who are looking for it haven't asked me yet where it was, and I ain't going to tell them.

II

We lived in a little one-room house with a fireplace. It was a room and a shed room that made the kitchen, and a gallery, or porch. They didn't call 'em porches then, called 'em galleries. We didn't have any screen doors, they hadn't been invented. You know, screen was one of the greatest inventions that ever happened? It kept the insects out of the house. And we had a water well and a hundred-acre farm, and I was the earliest one of the grandchildren of a big family. My grandmother, and my aunts and uncles and so forth, kind of ruint me, so they said, kind of give me the big head. My grandmother's house wasn't so far, and when I was two or three years old I'd run off and go over there. Our Aunt Jennie [Mary Virginia Bonner] lived with her, and she spoilt me too. She'd had me performing all kinds of big-head stunts. She had me get up on a stump when people would come and sing a song. I never did know what the song was, not the words to it, but it had a lot of "dibby-dibby-dabs," or something, in it.

Papa [William Henry Moore] farmed some, and fished in the wintertime, and we fished in the summer on the river, and would sell the fish to T. J. Taylor, and eat some of 'em. Course, them days, you didn't have any refrigeration at all. I was thirty-eight years old before I lived where there was electric power, and older than that before I had running water. We all was rich, or poor, whichever you want to call it. Everybody had the same thing, which was mostly nothing! We had a horse and a mule and a wagon and a buggy, and one time we had a surrey for a while. And we had hogs in the woods, we kept 'em up in the summertime, and we had cows in the woods that run out all year. We kept the crops fenced. We'd milk some of the cows and put the milk down in the well to keep it cool until our well caved in. Then we had to haul water from a spring for several years. Papa raised some cotton, corn, and peas, and always had a pretty good garden. We had plenty to eat, I reckon.

When I think about it, nearly everything we got now wasn't heard of then—telephone, TV, electricity, car, motorboat. A double-bit ax and a shotgun was the mainest tools a person had, and a squirrel dog. You would build a house, them days, with a double-bit ax and a broad ax and an auger to bore a hole for something.

As soon as I grew up a little, I began to go to the river with my step-grandpa Adams [Benjamin Franklin Adams]. I never actually knew any of my real grandparents much, except Papa's mother. Anyway, we'd go to the river, and that was ten years before the dam was built. My grandpa had a skiff down there, and he told me it was his lake. I guess he knew he was joking, but far as I knew it was his lake, because we never would see anybody else down there. The next grandchild after me was "Crip" Haddock [Floyd Haddock], and Crip would go with us. He had paralysis while he was four years old, but I can remember him walking to the lake with us, so it must have been before then. I'd have been about five, maybe six.

I remember the hogs would roost under the house in the wintertime, and Mama would heat some hot water on the fireplace and pour it through the cracks in the floor and make 'em leave. They'd leave in a hurry, sometimes they'd shake the whole house!

One time, some of the children had button shoes, and they'd got kind of damp and Mama stuck 'em in the oven of the wood cookstove after she cooked dinner one day and left 'em to gradually dry out. But she forgot 'em when she went to cook again, and them shoes curled up. I remember how they looked. They was just charcoal when she found 'em.

Another time, the old yellow tomcat would get in the stove when it was nearly cool for warmth. She accidentally shut him up in there one day and scorched him, but he got out in time. He squawled!

We had hogs and chickens and everything like that around, and we did our own churning. Mama would put us kids to churning there in the shedroom kitchen that had a door to the west end of it. We had hogs, and there was this old sow who would walk around in that backyard and turn her nose up and sniff this churn. One day Mama had me churning in the kitchen, and she'd warned me that hog would come in there to that churn if I didn't watch it. Anyway, I was churning away and thought of something I needed to go do right bad and went off for two or three seconds, seem like. Then I heard something rattle and I went back and this old hog had the churn over her head and was walking around the backyard with it. And there was the whole two days' milking—churn, butter, and everything—gone forever. It was a calamity.

I remember Papa making cough syrup. He'd take some rich pine, and get it afire in the fireplace, and hold it up, and hold a piece of fat meat over it, and the hot grease would run down in a can. Then they'd put maybe a little sweetening in it. The idea was to get the tar or turpentine out of this rich pine wood, mix it with the grease and sweetening, and we'd take that for cough syrup.

Somebody asked me the other day when did I start drinking. Well, I started when I was about eight years old. A cousin of Papa's, Mart Haley, would come by the house on a horse. We all thought a lot of Mart. He lived way down on the state line. He'd leave there on this horse and go to Marshall, then come back by our house and spend the night and make it on back home. But he brought some whiskey one time, and while Mama was cooking supper he got to giving me and my brother some little sips of the whiskey. When suppertime came, we set on a bench behind the table against the wall where there was a window. And I had a special plate somebody had give me, with flowers on it, and Mama would always put my plate there. Anyway, this time I gets back there raring around and standing up and fell overboard and broke my plate! That was my first episode of drinking something and I didn't drink no more until I was eighteen. I quit for ten years.

And I can recall before I was ten years old, we would go to Mr. Boehringer's [Gottleif Boehringer] down at Taylor Island. That was a big event. We'd go in the buggy, and on Taylor Island then there wasn't a bridge, so we'd have to cross a slough with about two feet deep of water in it. The old mule would wade it and the water would splash up in the buggy. Me and my brother Buddy, who was a couple of years younger than me, would sit down in the bottom of the buggy and enjoy crossing that slough. Mr. Boehringer was a fine person to visit. He entertained his guests lavishly, and he had plenty of wild meat and hogs and fish and stuff. In fact, he had a wire net fence built from Goose Prairie clear across to Annie Glade, and a whole area down there fenced-in hog-proof. Course, the lake was one bank of it, and some of the hogs would leave, but he'd keep most of 'em. He was kind of a hog baron down there, and would kill hogs and bring 'em to his butcher shop in Marshall.

Well, Papa liked to go down there because Boehringer served drinks, and when we started home some evenings Papa would just barely be able to sit in the seat of the buggy, and Mama would drive the old mule. The mule would be in a hurry to get home, and we'd go through the slough lickety-split and knock water every which-a-way. It tickled us kids. And then we'd hit roots around that rough road on the way home and that buggy look like it jumped three, four feet high! We'd get home and pour Papa in the bed and that was another big event in our day.

One time, Papa and Mike "Buckskin" Jones, our colored hired hand, spent all day going down to Boehringer's on Taylor Island and getting some hogs. Well, they brought the hogs home, and as usual they'd got drunk. They was unloading 'em up in back of our house where the barn was, and the hogs was squealing and taking on. Mama was in the house quivering because Papa was going to come in drunk directly. Then the horse and the mule run away and scattered hogs all down in front of the house and around.

Anyway, they got 'em straightened up. One of them pigs was a little spotted-looking pig, and it wasn't long till this pig was milking our cows. Did you know a hog will milk a cow? I've had it happen more than once. Once at the lake I had some pigs get started on sucking cows, milk cows. And they'll bite the tits. They've got little old sharp teeth and don't intend to bite them, but they do.

Boehringer kind of wanted to be different, I guess. He kept two bears down there, one of 'em old "Cuffin' Dan," two black bears on a leash. Papa told me he was riding in the woods squirrel hunting with a little dog and rode up to the Boehringer place, and there was nobody there. Papa said that his little squirrel dog was sniffing around them bears, looking at 'em, maybe barking at 'em. They was leashed to this table with a chain to their collars where they could go to the lake and come back up to their sleeping quarters. The bears kept piddling around, smelling the ground like they wasn't paying no attention to the dog. Finally, the dog got fairly close to 'em and this one bear run at him and throwed his hind foot out and grabbed at the dog. The bear realized that he could reach further with his hind foot from the end of the chain. A varmint like that gets pretty smart, someways.

And Boehringer had a bunch of big old dogs. I remember how they looked. I don't know what brand they were, maybe some German brand, but he had these woods full of hogs and hunted hogs with 'em.

You know, back in Germany wild boar hunting was a big sport. I can't recall that Boehringer put on any big show with boar hunting his hogs in the woods, but he had a bunch of guns, some of 'em muzzle-loaders, and he did run hogs with dogs and shoot 'em, either for his own amazement or maybe with his friends. He may just have had the old German idea of being a wild boar hunter, which is what the high-ups over there done. He probably in Germany wasn't high enough to hunt the "Fatherland" where they hunted wild boar, so he established him a domain over here of his own.

Boehringer could be rough. One time, my friend Jimmy Hall went down there and got on a drinking spell with Boehringer and they got in a fight and Jimmy cut him with a knife. Jimmy was a little short Irishman. He had his horse tied down at the lake, and when he cut him he run for old Prince. He had a saddle but had pulled the saddle off him and didn't have time to put it on. So he mounted old Prince and laid down on him holding on to his mane and circled the house while old man Boehringer started shooting at him with a Winchester.

The neighbors tell some scary tales about it. They say them bullets was glancing by and old Prince was running and Jimmy was over on the far side riding like an Indian, holding on with one foot up on his back and his arms around the mane. And they say when Jimmy went across the slough, he went across it so fast it parted the water and it was a day and a half 'fore it run back together!

Old Benny Jerry, who used to tell me some tales, said he owed Mr. Jimmy five dollars, and when he seed him coming up in the woods he had the money and thought he'd pay him, and tried to flag him down. He said he couldn't stop him. He waved a five-dollar bill at him, but Jimmy kept on riding.

I finally got to staying with my grandmother a whole lot when I was nine or ten years old. That's when my grandpa had died and left what he called a chest. Grandpa's chest was a secret that nobody hardly ever got to look in until he died. My grandmother would let me look in there at his things, and he had things you would mold buckshot with, and bullets. I guess he had had a muzzle-loader sometime, but when he died he left a big old ten-gauge double-barrel shotgun and a couple of boxes of New Club shells. Well, my grandmother would let me ride old Ruby, the horse, down to the river after school in the evenings. I'd be staying over there while Raymond Summers was on the lake fishing, and I'd ride down around where Caddo Lake State Park is now. It would be getting cool weather and they'd be a few ducks around about. The pond in the park and all those little inland lakes would be dried up, and they'd be separate from the river, and they'd be a lot of snakes had gathered to this puddle-hole as the water dried up. Varmints would eat a lot of 'em, and when it come cold weather, for some reason, those snakes would crawl out on the bank and get up beside a stump or something and ball up like earthworms in a ball big as a water bucket. And I'd shoot a hole through 'em with that ten-gauge double-barrel. That would confiscate most of 'em!

Then I trapped a good deal along pretty early, because that was the only way we had of getting a little income. I know I needed a .22 rifle. I wanted a .22 rifle and convinced myself I needed one. It went on for several years that we were trying to get me a .22 rifle, and one spring, Papa come to town in the wagon, and I went with him, and I was to get that rifle that day. My uncle, Perry Bonner, had some money in the bank, and he had told Papa that he'd loan him $125 to make a crop on. Well, someway or other Mama had wrote the check on Uncle Perry Bonner, who lived with us most of the time, but we got to the bank and they wouldn't cash it. So we didn't get any groceries for the summer, and we didn't get any rifle either, and we went back home. That was a kind of uneventful day.

But I finally got me a little .22 rifle, and I shot it a long time, killed lots of game with it, squirrels and things. Now, after being a member of the National Rifle Association for fifty years, and learning all about ballistics and how fast a bullet goes, and what it'll kill, and what kind you ought to have for certain game, and all, I can look back and see how lucky I was that I didn't know that stuff when I had my little .22 short. 'Cause I believed it would kill anything from a rat to an elephant. I guess I'd have shot an elephant with it. I know I used to shoot alligators and wonder why it didn't kill 'em. Course, I know now.

In 1908 we had awful high water. I've checked the records in the Shreveport Weather Bureau and the river went to forty-five feet at Shreveport. That don't mean much to some people, but the river hangs around seventeen or eighteen feet normally and it went up to forty-five feet. It washed the railroad away about two miles towards Jefferson from our farm, and the night train plunged into this creek. The engine made it across, but fell back in it. It killed one dead of the train crew, and hurt the others bad. They brought the passengers and some of the crew down to Karnack, and Mr. Baker, who lived near the railroad, fixed 'em breakfast. Somebody had one of the first inboard motorboats, a little one-cylinder, hand-cranking, flywheel, hot-shot-battery ignition boat, and loaded the hurt people, and the dead one too, I think, in the boat and carried them to Jefferson by water.

About that time I saw my first automobile down there towards Port Caddo. It had bicycle-looking wheels on it, and it had a little hand-cranking engine under the seat with some bicycle sprocket chains run back to the hind wheels. It didn't have a steering wheel, but had a lever that went down through the floor of this little surrey-looking rig and hooked to a rod that worked the front wheels. I was mechanically inclined and was observing all that.

The next car I remember seeing came by our house, which was about a mile from Karnack on the Marshall road. I was over across the way. A family of colored folks lived over there, and I was too little to plow, but one of the older boys, Jeff, would let me plow. He was letting me plow when this car come down the road and we heard it, and it turned over in front of our house. It didn't kill anybody out-right, but they got 'em up to the house. Old Dr. Baldwin was off down the road somewhere, and he come directly in a little two-horse gig he had. Well, when them horses seen that car upside down they whirled around and run out through the woods! I don't remember how they got the people to town, but one of 'em died. The other was a railroad man who talked about how long he'd run his engine on the railroad and never had an accident, and then get out in one of them blamed automobiles and nearly get killed.

III

That was getting up close to pearl-hunting days. The first dam on Caddo Lake didn't altogether end the pearl boom. The market simply declined since World War I was brewing in Europe. As I see it, the markets for pearls was to the emperors and empresses and the Kaisers and the Wilhelms. The royalty of Europe were the pearl buyers. They were trying to see which one of their wives could wear the biggest string of pearls.

A man named Teel and one named Allen found a pearl. Apparently there was some pearl hunting going on before in Arkansas on the White River. Anyway, Teel and Allen shipped it somewhere, maybe Tiffany in New York, and got money back for it. Then news kind of leaked out and people began to find pearls. Buyers began to show up. They would come on the train, the Kansas City Southern train, to Mooringsport, or they would come on motorboats. This was before the dam was built, and the water was low. It was considered a feat of navigation to take a motorboat up through the lake without running on shallow water and getting stuck. They'd follow the old river channel, see? One of the boats that the pearl buyers came up in was named the *Merry Widow*. It was a big old boat and would make a big wave. Us kids thought it was big fun to be out in the river when it passed in a skiff to feel it go up and down. One of the buyers was named Dr. Owens. Dr. Owens carried a satchel like the railroad conductors used to carry, one of them kind that, when you set it down, will fold up if there ain't nothing in it. He'd carry that full of money, and apparently nobody ever thought of robbing him. You know, when a fellow's buying stuff and he'll display a lot of money he'll get all the business. Dr. Owens would buy them, and, I imagine, take them to New York to sell.

There was various colored freshwater pearls. Some of them they called "buttons," and were kind of flat. Some of them was round. Sometimes you'd find what you call a "peeler." It was a dull-looking pearl. You could look at it and see where it was not developed smooth. Some people got proficient with a sharp knife at peeling that outer shell off of them and finding a fine little pearl inside. But some of 'em peeled out and nothing was in there—they got worse as you peeled 'em, you see. The gamble was, was you a real good judge of whether something would peel out of it or something wouldn't? In gathering mussels you'd find a good many kind of slug-looking things in there that had formed oblong or irregular and had a little glisten to 'em. They'd started to be pearl, but something had happened.

There were five or six different kinds of mussels on the bottom. There was some little kind of short, thin-shelled mussels we called "hickory nuts." There was another white-looking, thin-shelled mussel called "sand whistlers." We'd find them mostly on sandy places and I see some along the river now. The main mussel was a black mussel, a hard-shelled mussel; they seemed to produce the best pearls. Then they found some they called "washboards," which were rather large black mussels and were also looked upon as being a better chance for finding a pearl. This hickory nuts and sand whistlers and thin-shelled mussels never had much in them. And if they did, it wouldn't be much good.

There were vast bunches of people who just went on a wagon to the lake and carried a cotton sack. They'd wade out and along the bank as the water dropped in the summer and pick up some that didn't stay in the water. The water went off and left them and the sun would crack them open. There's been pearls found in mussels that had cracked open from the sunlight. Then they'd go out in shallow water and wallow along there and gather some in a sack and drag 'em to the bank and open 'em. Then on out deeper, where the water is, say, two or three feet deep, you'd just carry your boat. Get out in your boat in some old clothes and just wallow along in the lake and feel

around, and if you found a stump you'd nearly always find some mussels around the root of it. Us kids thought it was great fun to go, because we liked to swim or get in the water. But after you stayed in
that hot water all day, it got to be monotonous.

Some people wading in the water a little too deep would feel for
'em with their feet, then stick their head under and pick them up by
hand. Others would rake the mussel on top of one foot with the
other and then lift the foot up. One old man named McCathern developed the idea of being comfortable while he hunted pearls, and
built what he called a "whangdoodle boat." It was a flat-bottomed
boat, maybe sixteen feet long. He put a wagon sheet over it and put
him a bed on it, a platform where he could hang his hands over the
back and hunt wherever he could reach bottom. One time, after he
had eaten dinner, which consisted of meat and biscuits and sweet potatoes, he was hunting along and drowsed off to sleep and a snake
swallowed one of his fingers! When he pulled his hand up, there was
a snake on it. The snake wasn't trying to bite him, it had just smelled
that grease on his finger and swallowed it. Then there was another
pearl hunter that had one arm off about four inches from the shoulder. He hunted with his other hand, and would go along there and be
under the water up to his chin, and would stick that nub up and wig-
gle it back and forth right fast. I don't know what was the purpose of
that—just entertaining people, I guess.

I don't exactly know where old man McCathern got his name for
the whangdoodle boat. There was a place called Whangdoodle Pass.
In fact, it has got now to be where there's two or three Whangdoodle
Passes, because people who thought they knew where the original
was got to calling different openings Whangdoodle. So now I'm not
sure which was the original. And then the Whangdoodle is about
played out. There's places on the lake like Whangdoodle Pass that
used to be used considerable, but are hardly ever used anymore.
There was Goose Prairie and Hog Wallow and Turtle Shell and Eagle's
Nest and Big Lake and Ames Spring Basin. A lot of the names are still
there, but some of 'em have through time that I remember drifted
into being called other places. There's Twin Islands and one they
called kind of an odd name, Pig Turd Island. I don't know how it got
that name. There's Clinton Lake, Carter Lake, Bird Roost, and the
main hole, or the deepest part of Clinton Lake, that was called the
Judd Hole. It was named after an old man called Judd, who was later
found dead in his camp somewhere down there.

The season for pearl hunting, of course, was in warm weather
when you could afford to get out in the water, and one of the main
gathering places was on the north shore because of the water situa-

tion. There was some springs over there called Ames Spring and Shoultz Spring where [Robert] Potter settled and was killed. People would come with their teams and wagons, and maybe an old wooden boat in the wagon, and tie the mules up and feed 'em out there and maybe water 'em. They took water for cooking, and so forth. They put the boat in the lake and camped on the bank at night. And sometimes, with a wagon sheet on the boat, the whole family would go along on the lake and camp overnight on the boat. I can remember looking down from Towhead Island there one day, and it looked like a hundred or more boats out there, a lot of 'em with shades, tops on 'em, generally wagon tops. Those days, nearly everybody had bows and wagon sheets to take and put on their wagon at times. A boat was about the right width to put up a couple of clips on it and a couple of bows and stretch a wagon sheet on it. You could get out of the hot sun under there. And with holes at both ends, it wasn't too hot. It created a little breeze through there that way.

I don't know of anybody who was too outstanding in finding any more pearls than the rest of us. "The Jap" [George Sachihiko Murata] did pearl hunt some, but he wasn't any more active than some of the rest of us. There was a lot of people who would go a day or two or three, and then give it up, go for something else. My dad would pearl hunt some through the summer, but he never was too much of a gambler about spending several days gathering mussels and finding nothing. He'd give up on it, but about the time he'd give up, somebody would find one. Of course that was incentive to continue.

People got twenty or thirty dollars for pearls on up to—the best I remember—maybe four or five hundred dollars, which was a lot of money. No taxes, no nothing. You could buy a sack of flour for a dollar, a turning plow for two dollars, and a mule for twenty-five dollars. So that was a lot of money. My dad-in-law took up buying pearls rather than hunting them, my wife's father, Charlie Hayner, and he dealt in 'em some.

Papa would go pearl hunting in the summer after we'd laid by our crop. He'd take me one day and then my brother Buddy [Vernon Hatley Moore] the next. We would go down towards Starr Ranch, which is now in the war plant [Longhorn Ordnance Plant], and cross Goose Prairie in the buggy there close to the Dallas Caddo Club. It'd be dry in them days. Then we'd go 'cross Starr Ditch and on to the back side of Pine Island, where we had an old wooden boat. Then we'd hunt out from there toward Towhead Island and around. One summer we camped a little on Towhead. I remember there was lots of big old cottonmouth water moccasins around that island, and up in the middle of the day the river would be way low, down like Sabine River would be, and we'd seine minnows over there on sandbars. They'd be big old black bullfrogs setting out there in the hot sun in the middle of the day, down next to the riverbank. They was a fellow there who had something we all wished we had. He came from Jefferson and was pearl hunting, and he had a sort of cot affair, a one-man bed, that had a wagon sheet frame built over it with little windows in it made out of mosquito bar material. It was a store-bought rig, probably from L. L. Bean in Maine or somebody. We'd fight mosquitoes all night and this fellow would get up in that little tent.

My Uncle George Bonner was pretty lucky at finding pearls, and you could tell when he had found one. On weekends, the biggest event in a pearl hunter's or fisherman's or Caddo Lake rat's life was to come around to Karnack and drink and shoot craps, play pittypat or pitch or poker over at the depot. Uncle George, when he had found a pearl, he'd be drinking and laughing. And he'd open up his pocketbook and hold it just where you could look way down in there and see a little bit of cotton. Then he'd shut it back right quick, and laugh. He'd say, "I've found a peach!"

But Uncle George got some pretty good money. He sold his pearls right across from Taylor Island near Boehringer's place. There was a sandbar there, and the pearl buyers then met over there on that sandbar, and that's where they sold the pearls.

Teel and Allen discovered the first pearls. I don't remember Teel, but Mr. Allen had granulated eyelids. His eyes were red, and he looked like he was powerful drunk all the time. He wasn't, but he was drunk a good deal of the time. Mr. Allen wouldn't go out in a boat much, he would take a cotton sack and wade around in the edge of the lake and wallow out there and gather mussels and put 'em in this cotton sack and drag 'em to the bank and open 'em. He used that method a good deal.

Well, it became customary over there, that if any of the gang found a pearl, he would carry four or five of his cronies to Shreveport, and they'd have a two-day party. They'd get down there and den up in the Belmont Hotel and range down in the St. Paul bottoms at night. That was before Prohibition, and they'd have a sure-enough big party with whoever it was's pearl money till it was gone. Frank Galbraith, my friend the boatbuilder, used to go with 'em.

But Mr. Allen would get snakes in his boots, get to having hallucinations. One morning they couldn't find him when they woke up; he wasn't in the hotel, and they went out to look for him. That was before the days of cars to any extent, and there was lots of horses in Shreveport. Texas Street was a horse-carriage road. They claim they found old man Allen, who was used to picking up mussels out in the lake and putting 'em in the cotton sack, out on Texas Street crawling down it on his all fours. He was picking up "horse apples" and breaking 'em open, and if he found a grain of corn, he'd put it in his pocket! Dreamed he was hunting pearls.

At the end of the pearl hunting boom, and after the dam raised the water, the Galbraiths, for one, and some of the Big Lake people down in there got them a long-handled garden rake, one that had the handle that instead of going directly into the rake spread out and went around to each side. It made a kind of fork that went to the rake. They'd put a wire basket behind it and dig along the bottom and attempt to shovel mussels into this basket. They gathered some that way, but the market fell off because of World War I and they just about quit fooling with it.

IV

You know how we'd get the weather report in the early days? We would listen for T-Model trucks coming through the night and decoy ducks a-quacking. Well, that'd be duck hunters coming to the lake. They would have had a weather report in Marshall by telegraph that a norther was coming. So next morning Papa would say, "Let's get up two or three hogs and kill 'em. It's gonna be cold weather here and a good time to kill hogs."

Along about then was when the first motorboats come, and my grandpa builded a boat down there on the side of the creek, close to where he lived, with Jake Adams, his boy. They put a little one-cylinder motor in it, a Detroit. It had a kind of a lever on it, and when the timer, the distributor we call 'em now, would play out on it, you could use a piece of the hoop off a cedar water bucket. It had a little vibrating coil and some hot-shot batteries, like on telephones.

· The Gray Marine Company also made a motor, and Mr. John Kelly from Marshall had a camp on the lake, and he had a one-cylinder, six-horsepower engine built by Gray. He bought it in 1906 and ran the thing until he died just a few years ago. It wore out so bad that the piston had done turned sideways in it. I told him about a machine shop down in Plaquemines, Louisiana, that was still making a motor similar to that, and he went down there a few years before he died and got 'em to make a crankshaft for this old motor that was built in 1906!

Them days there wasn't any outboards at all—strictly inboards. I don't remember an outboard until around 1917 or 1918, when Evinrude and Johnson come along. I know the first little Johnson wasn't very popular here because it had a shear pin in it, and if you hit the least bit of an obstruction it would shear. Then you'd have to take your propeller off and put this pin back in it. Later they got to putting clutches in 'em where you could bounce over a stump and keep going.

Some of the events of those early days—there was the big blowout in the oil fields and the coming of Halley's comet. Jake Adams went to work over in the oil fields at Oil City about then, and when they's drilling over there they had several blowouts. One of 'em caught fire down near the bank of the lake, and for a year or more one of the landmarks of the country was the burning well. They'd be people gather up late in the evening and go down there from Uncertain in a motorboat to observe this gas burning. It was quite a fire; you could even see the light from Karnack. I've heard the old buffalo fishermen say they'd trammel net around there up and down the bank by the light of it, and that you could feel the warmth of it clear out on the lake. It left a barren place over there for years where it had burned. I guess it just finally went out itself.

And Halley's comet come along about then and I saw it a few times. One of the times I can particularly remember was late in the evening when we were going to church, or maybe prayer meeting. We were down close to Mr. Baker's house and could see up the road west from there, and by a little after dark we could see Halley's comet. Apparently it was traveling north, and it left a kind of trail of light back from it to the south. That was about 1910. You could see it a week or two before it disappeared. You know it's due back in a few years? Wonder if I can go back down there where I saw it about seventy-five years ago and see it again?

I just happened to think about the bad luck signs we used to have when we were kids. I never heard of any good luck signs. One of 'em was that it was bad luck to bring a hoe in the house, and one day Mama had company, and us kids was playing, and I run through the house with a hoe. I went through the second time before she noticed it, and all at once they discovered me there with a hoe and shut me down. One of the neighbors suggested that if you took the hoe back out the same door you come in, it would take the hex off you. So she ordered me out the door, but after I got out I told her, "I come in that other door!" So they all just give up and resigned themselves to die. Well, Mama lived to be ninety-one and I'm eighty-two, so the hex didn't work on us.

I remember my wife's grandmother, Mrs. Blair. When she'd see a black cloud coming she'd run out in the yard and stick a double-bit axe in the ground, leave one blade sticking up, and say, "That'll split the cloud!" Split the cloud and make it go around each side of us.

Then if a screech owl screeched at night, that was bad luck, and if a hen crowed you'd better not let her crow again. Mama never would let her crow but once—she'd have chicken and dumplings made of her!

And I was thinking about the old-time peddlers from them days. You'd see one coming down the road on a hot day in the dust, kind of wiping his face, and he'd be carrying something look like a bale of cotton. He'd have a dry-goods store on his back! He'd get to the house and spread it out there, lay it on chairs and on the bed and on the floor, and it'd look like a whole dry-goods store in there. We'd, I guess, buy something sometimes, and once or twice one of the peddlers spent the night at our house. Some of the peddlers had a jewelry department, a little velvet-lined box with a lock on it that they'd open up to display these diamonds and necklaces and gold and silver and stuff, or whatever it was. There was also peddlers that come through the country in wagons and buggies, with a few chickens tied on. I don't know just what all they had. There was an old gentleman named John Hill, who was crippled in one arm, and he traveled in one of these Conestoga wagons with a wagon sheet on it and a stove in it with a stovepipe sticking out the back. He just prowled through the country. I remember he borrowed a wagon wheel from Mr. Henry Hall once, claimed his had broke down somewhere up the road, and it was two years before Henry got his wagon wheel back.

That was about the time Papa got to be constable. We had a colored boy named Mike Jones, who was our farmhand and bodyguard. We named him "Buckskin," because buckskin was his color. He was eight or ten years older than us seven- or eight-year-old kids, and would pull us in the red wagon and go hunt bird nests with us. And when Papa was off constabling, why Mike would plow and my brother Buddy and I would both chop a little cotton.

Mr. Will Baldwin was the justice of the peace and lived up the Marshall road a ways. But there was a road across the woods we called the Taylor Cutoff off toward Leigh, and the saloons were still in Leigh at that time. Karnack had voted out whiskey. Anyway, they'd always hold court at Leigh on Saturday where the liquor was. Papa had a little yellow horse he'd ride down there, but sometimes he'd have to lead her home. If he didn't get home by midnight, Mama would send the Buckskin off down the Leigh road to hunt him. In later years, the Buckskin, Mike, told me he had met Papa a time or two when he was still trying to get on old Daisy, his saddle horse, and wasn't able to. They'd both finally get on her and ride her home.

Anyway, they'd pretty soon collect enough fines at the court to go to the saloons and start celebrating. They had one colored boy in that country named Jimmy Crenshaw. I don't know, there probably wasn't nothing wrong with him, but he'd get reported lots for crap-shooting or fighting or something, and pretty often he'd be one of the victims of the trial at Leigh on Saturday and would pay enough of a fine for them to get the liquor. One time I guess Papa got over-anxious and captured him along in the middle of the week for some infraction, and was going to save him for Saturday. Papa was gone somewhere and had Jimmy locked in the cotton house. I think he had him hand-cuffed or something. Anyway, about the middle of the morning, Mike, the Buckskin wage-hand, come told Mama, "Jimmy's done picked his lock!" Mama went out in the backyard where Papa had a workbench with a vise on it and started cleaning vegetables out there like she just happened to do it, but she was really watching the barn. Mama had one of Papa's pistols out there too, for bluff, I guess. But finally Jimmy crept out of the barn and walked real slow and on tiptoe until he got to the fence. Then he stepped over it right quick and pulled his cap off and went through the woods. Mama shot the pistol up in the air. Stories got out about how she creased his hat, and all, but that was just a joke.

But Jimmy was gone, and it went on maybe two or three months that they didn't have Jimmy to depend on. One Friday morning Papa got up and I noticed him putting some ears of corn in a sack, and some fried meat and biscuits in another sack, and some baked-yesterday sweet potatoes in there for a lunch, and he left. He was gone all of that day and that night, but the second night he come in, sometime way in the night. He'd went over into Louisiana around Gilliam and got the local constable to help him and they captured Jimmy. Then he'd locked a chain around Jimmy's neck and the other end around old Daisy, the wild horse's neck, and he rode and let Jimmy walk back. He told Jimmy, says, "Now, you get to trying to run off, you'll make old Daisy get scared and she'll run away and kill all three of us." I don't know what the extradition procedures were. I guess they let the horse decide when they got to the state line. But anyway, the next morning he had Jimmy locked to a tree and Papa's reputation for extradition done got built up across the countryside.

Buckskin Mike Jones, that worked for us, Papa would let him squirrel hunt on Saturdays. I don't know where he went, he talked like he come down around Taylor Island, but he'd bring in a bunch of cat squirrels in a sack. Us kids would admire 'em, and he'd hold 'em up and explain the conditions under how he killed each one of 'em. That was a great thing to listen to. "This un here was goin' up a certain big tree or was runnin' on the ground, or what, and I popped him." Papa had a lever-action ten-gauge shotgun Buckskin would hunt with. The gun was nearly big as Buck was, and I imagine that if you shot anyways near 'em you could hit 'em. One time, blackbirds flew around the house on a cold winter day, and Papa went out there when they flew up and shot in 'em with this ten-gauge shotgun, and so many of 'em fell the rest of 'em thought the flock was lighting! So they come back and he shot in 'em again till he shot three or four times. We had blackbirds all over the field.

We'd eat 'em, too. Sometimes we shot redbirds and thrush. I'd hunt them thrush with a .22 rifle up and down a little creek ravine, and dress 'em and bring 'em home, and Mama would put some dumplings with 'em and cook 'em. Them redbirds and thrush and robins all got good light meat.

We kids used to make a "flying jenny." We'd find us a stump and put a board on top of it and nail a big nail down through it, then nail a board on the end of this long board and put a couple of the littlest kids astraddle of it, and let them lock their arm around it. Then we'd whirl 'em, see if we could sling 'em off. You could get up a pretty good momentum with two people whirling this flying jenny. Those flying jennies would kill you!

And we walked "tom walkers" [stilts] and rolled hoops and popped the whip. At school we'd take the biggest kids and let them be at the end, and the next one would hold to their hand to their hand to their hand till you got a string of 'em, down to some of the littlest ones. Put them on the end of it. Then you'd run, and the big ones would stop, pull that row of kids back, and that far end would whip around there and sling that last kid about fifty feet out through the woods. Great sport!

Besides entertaining ourselves with them homemade games, we had to milk the cows, feed the mules, plow the crops, cut wood for the fireplace and the cookstove, shell peas, and put up peaches in the summer. Dry 'em on top of the house and mix chinaberry leaves with 'em to keep the bugs out, then sack 'em up for winter. No refrigeration, no electricity, no gas, no car—the good old days kind of case-hardened you, I guess, for these progressive times we live in now.

Then I started going to school, and there was a man lived over in the country a ways had a good hunting dog, a big old redbone hound. And we spent most of our time going to school towards the end of the week trying to catch this old dog to hunt with that weekend. We'd catch her at the schoolhouse and tie her over in a little creek bottom. Then maybe some of the other boys would steal her away from us. But whoever wound up with her at the end of the week would get to go hunting that weekend and catch some varmints and sell the hides.

Around them days, there would be a Mr. Bell come from town in a buggy with the fattest horse I ever saw. Francis Bell and a big stout boy named Robertson would come down the road carrying their camping equipment in the buggy and walking. Our water well was there with a trough where you could water your horses, and was pretty close to the road. They would stop and water the horse and draw a bucket of water, and this Robertson, who was a stout boy like, bigger than me, he'd pick this whole water bucket up and drink out of it. I admired him! I'd always, as I grew up bigger, go out there and see if I was able to hold the bucket up with two hands and drink out of it.

When we were kids at home then, we had younger brothers and sisters coming on, but Buddy and I were several years older than the next child, and we were together a whole lot. We wasn't too old when Buddy and I learned how to build wire nets and acquired us a bicycle. We'd put a pole from the handlebars of one bicycle to the saddle of the other through the wire net, and we'd haul 'em to the river on back north of where we lived, which is now through the state park. Pretty soon, we had us a little fishing arrangement going on down there.

Once, me and Buddy was hunting down through the bottoms in the park and he got snakebit. A ground rattler bit him; I killed the snake. It wasn't far from the lake, so I got Buddy in a motorboat that was there that belonged to my uncle, and I tried to crank it to take him down to Port Caddo where I could get him first aid. It'd probably be easier to have brought him home, but I thought this would give me a good excuse to use the boat. But I never could get it started; it'd just hit a lick and quit. I guess I probably didn't turn the gas on. Well, I finally had to start home with him, and his leg swelled up so I was carrying him when I got half home. There was a neighbor there, a Mr. Blair, and I prevailed upon him to get a horse to carry Buddy on home. Didn't have any coal oil—had to go to Karnack to get coal oil before we could soak his leg. He stayed swelled up quite a while.

Once, I was with Buddy when it came an eclipse about four o'clock in the evening. We was plowing over there in the field and we un-hooked the mules and went home. The mules knew it was time to go home, and the chickens was even going to roost! But Papa made

Buddy and me go back to the fields, it was three hours till dark in the summertime, and plow some more. Sun came back out in about forty minutes.

And one time we had a railroad, Buddy and I. Along when we was twelve or thirteen years old, we found some handcar wheels off up the railroad in a creek bed—four wheels and two axles. The wheels was solid on the axles and had a sprocket on 'em where the handcar thing run. We rolled 'em down the railroad to our pasture land that adjoined it back in behind the farm, and one Saturday when we were supposed to be hauling wood we hauled 'em home. There was a kind of an incline up behind our house through the woods, a pretty good little hill. We took those wheels up there and builded us a flatcar affair. Then we made track out of everything we could find, all the loose lumber. We had a little section made out of brick, some made out of bed rails, and then we got in such a tight for trackage that we hewed some little pine trees in the woods and made track. We'd roll that little handcar up the hill, push it by hand, then ride it back. One time, when Papa and Mama were gone on a Sunday and Papa had some lumber laying there to build a barn, we grabbed up all the lumber and the rest of the kids in the country and run the line all the way down to the big road. We had a brake on each side, one for each of us to hold, but that thing would get to rolling fast, and was dangerous.

Finally, one time, Papa left to go to town and ordered Buddy and I to go to a certain part of the cotton field and start picking cotton. Well, we went up to the railroad to spend a few minutes there, but we got to studying and planning and engineering the fact that we might put in a switch, where we could throw the switch and run off the main line over on a spur, and we forgot about time. Look like it hadn't been for a few minutes, but it'd been two or three hours. We looked up, and Papa was getting out of the car down in front of the house! We grabbed our cotton sacks and took off to the cotton patch, and we was picking over there when we heard a ringing sound, kind of like bells a-ringing. I suspected what it was. When we got home that evening both wheels on one side of our railroad car were scrambled with a sledge hammer. That settled our railroad venture, and we sold out to a junk man that was traveling in a hack buggy with a big old dock-tailed horse. We got twenty cents for what was left of our railroad, a dime apiece.

Papa built houses up at the Wurtsbaugh mill for the workman to stay in, and I would go with him one day as a helper, and Buddy would go the next. Wurtsbaugh was a German and a sawmill man. He'd established quite a sawmill just five miles up the track from

Karnack towards Jefferson on Haggerty Creek. There was quite a lot of timber available around the mill, and he also had a large tract of land that lay near the river between Karnack and Uncertain. He built a steel railroad out of Karnack to about four miles along the river, and had a little dinky sawmill engine and flatcars here. They'd cut those timbers down next to the river and haul 'em with this little dinky engine up to the main line. Then the local freight would carry 'em the five miles to the sawmill and set 'em off. Then they'd drag 'em into a lake, which kept 'em from drying out, and had a wagon-looking affair that backed down a ramp into the water to get 'em. This wagon bed had a cable on it that run out onto the sawmill floor.

The mill was along the railroad, and they had a grocery store there, a commissary, and would pay the millhands off in chips. T. J. Taylor here in Karnack would take chips, but would get a discount on them when you cashed 'em in. One day the sawmill men were all eating dinner at Karnack and the little dinky steam engine was setting down on the tracks. Then they looked around and saw it was moving. The throttle had worked open. There was a man who kept a horse that rode down on the "front," as they called it in them days [the cutting zone of the lumbering operation], and he lit out on the horse to catch it. The engine kept getting faster, but he finally overtook it up on the field a ways and got on and shut it down. If it had went on down to the river it probably would have jumped the track.

I remember the man, named Westbrook, who was "head knocker" up there. They'd saw lumber and ship it north. They'd bring in a load of logs and wait until the local freight brought some flatcars empty and set 'em off, then they'd go back to the woods with these flatcars after another load of logs.

One time the engineer and fireman was laying down under the shade of a tree waiting on the local freight, and this big old Injun was sitting there on this log road track. There was a couple of hoboes that got off it, young kids and one of 'em real blond-headed. They was eyeing this Injun up and down, and asked the engineer who was reading the paper, says, "Mister, what road is this?" The engineer didn't even look up. He said, "Son, this is the SH & IT, the Shreveport, Houston and Indian Territory."

Along about 1908 or 1909, after the first dam was built, the government maintained a boat on the lake, a houseboat, called the "snagboat." It was something like twenty feet wide by maybe sixty or seventy feet long, with little houses down each side, and a hallway through the middle and a kitchen in the back. When they moved, they pulled it with skiffs and oars on down the river.

It was manned by Captain Clark and a crew of about five. It would camp up and down the river and hire local young men to work. They didn't pay much, but they had awful good groceries, they had board. The men would use axes and things to cut debris off the bank and dynamite tree tops out of the river. It was kind of an aftermath of the steamboat days, I guess. Papa would go to the lake on the days they were going to dynamite and gather fish that would be killed when they blew tops. Once, when they were in Jefferson, they were trying to blow a log out of the river and tried it a time or two and it didn't go. A fellow, Hayner, one of my wife's uncles, said he would get rid of it. He put enough dynamite under it that it blowed the log out of the river and hit the corner of a brick building in uptown Jefferson!

And don't many people remember it, but the Caddo Lake Dam broke about 1912 or 1913. There was a slab of about eighty feet long fell out. Water run over the top and eroded the lower side, and the chunk fell out and left an opening. Well, the Gulf Oil Company immediately put machinery there, drag lines and what-have-you, and drove a crescent-shaped barricade above this break. Then they drove another barricade a short distance off from it, about thirty or forty feet, and filled the in-between with sandbags, rocks, and everything they could get ahold of to stop the break from leaking.

It was maybe two years before the Corps of Engineers put a permanent patch in the dam, and there was quite an industry developed up around Karnack. The Corps of Engineers taken it upon themselves to dig big barge loads of rock, one after the other, out of the State Park area and haul it down to the dam to re-enforce it.

Of course, it wasn't much of a dam anyway. It was only a dam to maintain a four-foot higher level on Caddo Lake than had been when it was just a natural lake. The way the natural lake was formed was that Red River rafted up and deposited silt and all, and got higher than the Caddo Lake area and it just pooled up here. When the steamboats were coming up, they were able to come on up to Jefferson because Red River would be high, and the log jam—the raft—made the water spread out all over the country and hold Cypress River up to Jefferson.

The tugboat for this rock hauling to the dam that was pulling the barges was the old *Senator Shepard* out of Jefferson. Senator Shepard was the senator from this area, and as far back as the late twenties, he would come to Jefferson sponsoring navigation, and show pictures of steamboats somewhere running, and tell about how they'd soon have 'em running again to Jefferson up Caddo Lake. Well, you'll know 'bout what the status of navigation to Jefferson is now! I'm still believing they're gonna do it, and I'm just wondering—I'm eighty-two—if they would hire a 150-year-old riverboat pilot? If they will, I might get a job.

V

But up until 1910 there wasn't a dam, and the Red River was blocked by logs and jams. When overflows came, it would pool back up in here and enormous amounts of buffalo and catfish apparently drifted here from Red River or Mississippi or anywhere in the whole United States. They would come up here and there were tons of 'em caught. Now, with the dam on the lake and its being a landlocked lake, it doesn't produce the catfish, buffalo, or carp that it used to.

Caddo Lake used to be quite a freshwater fishery. Mr. T. J. Taylor here in Karnack, Lady Bird Johnson's father, was a shipper of fish. There was four passenger trains a day here then, two in the day and two in the night. About two days a week, Tuesdays and Fridays, was fish-delivering days, and the trains would sometimes be an hour and a half loading fish on the express cars. They'd be eight or ten of those express fish wagons loaded with barrels of fish packed in ice to ship to Dallas, Greenville, and on up north of here—maybe some into Oklahoma and Shreveport. The lake would furnish enormous amounts of fish.

One day Mr. Taylor shipped 5,200 pounds of white perch and carp. That would go on about seven or eight months of the year, mostly through the winter and spring. And next year you could put your nets back in there and catch 'em by the boatloads again. Once, an uncle of mine that I was fishing on shares with had 1,800 pounds of white perch, more white perch than people get to see these days in a lifetime. Things do change around.

The status of the commercial fishing was, that back at the turn of the century there were people, natives, around that farmed in the summer and fished some on maybe Saturdays, and all. Old man T. J. Taylor began to handle fish. Those days there wasn't any transportation from Marshall down here, just a buggy and wagon road, but Marshall was beginning to grow with the Texas and Pacific shops, things moving ahead, and there developed quite a market in Marshall for fish. Papa would sometimes carry a load in the wagon—he'd buy some and catch some—and my uncle, Perry Bonner, was one of the top four or five biggest fishermen. He would invest a thousand or so dollars in hoop nets for the winter, and I'd fish with him on shares. He'd give me six or eight nets, then I'd help him and he'd help me. We had a log cabin down there on the lake that he had built. There were two rooms to it with a hallway between them, but the hallway wasn't floored. One room had a fireplace in it, and on real cold days we would cook on the fireplace in frying pans. We had a dutch oven for cooking bread and it worked good. On medium days we would cook out in the open hallway under the shed if it was rainy. If it got better weather, then we'd move right out in the yard.

We camped on the lake down at Swanson's Landing—me, my Uncle Perry Bonner, George and Raymond Summers, "Shine" Hale, and Eugene Hayner. And on fish-delivering mornings we'd get up about three or four o'clock down there and go dip up what fish we had, three or four or five hundred pounds of white perch, and maybe some catfish and buffalo, and deliver 'em here to Karnack.

We'd get up so early we wouldn't eat any breakfast before we left. The idea was to get here and get the fish to Karnack in time to load 'em on the train at nine-thirty or ten o'clock. So we had a deadline to meet, and we'd dip up them fish and then pull 'em the five or six miles from down there up here with oars through the lake. Maybe it would be pretty good weather, or maybe foggy, but the way we navigated through the fog was to listen at the pump station over yonder. The rule was to keep that pump station towards your left oar, then you'd hit somewhere up in here around Goose Prairie and get there.

Anyway, we'd get 'em on a fish truck after we weighed 'em and go home. I'd get home about nine o'clock in the morning—hadn't eat anything since the day before. Well, Mama would always have left-over biscuits, and we had sorghum syrup or ribbon cane syrup, some kind of syrup. I remember one time we didn't have any butter but Mama had Snowdrift lard, and I'd eat that Snowdrift lard on the biscuits and syrup, and it was real good.

We'd deliver on Monday or Tuesday, and again on Friday, and one morning my uncle and me had them 1,800 pounds of white perch. It'd take an hour and a half at Karnack to load 'em on the train. They'd ship 'em up the railroad to Dallas and Greenville, and haul some locally to Marshall and Longview. Marshall was a pretty good market for buffalo fish, the carp-like fish we'd catch trammel-netting. The fishermen who fished mostly through the winter farmed a little through the summer. In summer the net fishing wasn't any good. Besides, we only had cotton nets those days, and they'd rot out pretty quick. We'd blister ourselves all over the place tarring 'em in the early fall—get out kind of hid in the woods somewhere and fire up a vat and tar the net and blister our face, nearly. Then we'd get 'em in the lake and they'd be sticky all the first winter. Some people, nearly all of 'em, kept trammel nets, and two people in one boat could run the trammel net. Trammel netting wasn't much good in the winter and hoop netting wasn't much good in the summer. Mr. Taylor would have a market for a couple of hundred pounds, whatever he wanted, and he'd give the orders to probably whoever owed him the most. Then they'd catch the fish. I remember a night we caught five hundred and some odd pounds and I made a little over seventeen dollars as a one-third-interest partner. The man who owned the net and the boat would get two-thirds and the help would get one-third. Well, that was pretty big money then.

Old man Taylor would order whatever hoop nets and materials for wings we needed, and we put those four-and-a-half-foot front, and eighteen-feet-long, two-throated barrels out, with a wing run from the middle of one barrel over to another barrel and each end tied to stumps. They were pretty expensive nets and they had to be tarred. Sometimes we would order 'em tarred and sometimes we'd order 'em white, and we had a tar vat to fire up to tar 'em. Kind of a messy operation—tar all over your boat through the winter and under your fingernails all the time.

Just put hoop nets out anywhere in Big Lake in the deep water there and they'd catch a pretty good wad of fish, sometimes a hundred white perch in each end of 'em. But there was always the possibility that the game warden would find one. In the spring it was customary around points of Big Green Brake and around other so-called points that was known as awful good sets to take a single-wing hoop net and put a single-barrel hoop on it and run it out from the bank just barely deep enough for the barrel to go under. We'd use an old net that didn't have much life in it, so, in case the warden got it, he wouldn't get much future use out of it. And sometimes it would catch an enormous amount of fish there for about three or four weeks in the spring.

The wings would have corks on top, and we would tie rocks or bricks on the bottom of it about every ten feet to pull the wing down to the bottom. Then the floats held the top of the wing up towards the surface. Usually the wing was about as high as the height of the barrel of the net, or slightly higher, about five or six feet. It would catch catfish and white perch. I remember not too many years ago catching 266 in one that I had stretched out down there. Then I decided to move that net one day over to another part of the lake. I put it on a skiff and tied my inboard to it and hurried over with it, but wasn't able to get it exactly where I wanted it. I put it out kind of temporary over in Louisiana. Then, a day or so later I happened to pick up a *Shreveport Times* and there was my net pictured across the front of it laying on the courthouse square in Shreveport! It told all

about who found it, and about how long and big it was, and what its
utmost enormous capacity to catch all the fish in the lake was. At
the bottom it said, "The arrest of the guilty party is imminent." But
it wasn't as imminent as they thought. They throwed a big spell of
hunting down there for nets even over in Texas, and I would go down
and watch them sloshing around out there.

Now in the spring, when fishing on the lake dwindled down, if we
got a spring rise we used to bring what we called "muleys" off up the
lake and put them out along the riverbank. These were single-barrel
hoop nets without wings, and we'd usually fish the oldest kind. My
wife's dad lived right here in Karnack and farmed a little and fished
the river for several years. He was careful about it and didn't advertise
himself. Along about February and on into the spring he'd haul some
pretty good wagonloads of fish with his old one-eyed horse out to
Mr. T. J. Taylor. He fished the muley, the single net, and he knew
some of the best places to put 'em. Finally, one Christmas Day, I was
around down there, and a warden, Breedlove, and another warden I
didn't know worked all day gathering those nets up the river and putting them on the bank and burning 'em. He never did go back in
business, but he'd made quite a bit of money out of it the ten or
twelve years he'd fished.

Through the winter, hoop netting was the most prevailing method
of fishing, but as spring came, you would fish a trammel net some if
the night was warm. A trammel net is a seventy-five- or eighty-yard
net that has leads on the bottom and corks on the top. It's about five
feet deep and consists of three walls of thread. The middle wall is a
small-mesh, light webbing. The outer walls are rather heavy twine
with about ten-inch mesh, and they match each other on each side.
The webbing on the inside would be seven-and-a-half feet deep if the
net itself was five feet deep, which was customary. A fish would run
into it from either side and push that small webbing inside through
the big mesh out the other side, and pocket himself. It was customary for people to fish the trammel nets through the summer.

Now, trammel netting wasn't gill netting. A gill net is just a straight
line of thread that a fish swims into, and when he backs out it hangs
in his gills. He'll try to get himself out and wrap himself up in it. I've
got some gill netting now. No, the methods of operation of the trammel net was kind of hard work. You had a wooden skiff with oars in it
and the back end was the net platform. The seat was made two-and-
a-half-foot wide from the back towards the front. You would fold this
net on it, flatten it down and fold it back and forth, and each end of
the net had two loops in it to stick a stick through. You would prowl
the banks of the lake, and when you found a good place you would

stick one stick down towards the bank. Then you'd make a circle and confine that circle, and go in there with a pole—a flail pole, we called it—and beat the water. Or maybe you'd have a pole with a cowbell on it that you'd stick down under the water and shake the cowbell and drive the fish into the net. You could seem 'em running and hitting it and sinking the corks. Some would jump over it and some would run to it and come back and wouldn't run into it. Then you'd take the net up and pull it in the boat, and fold it back again, and sort of shake that middle webbing down towards the top when you put it out again. You'd make twenty-five or thirty of those sets through the night and it turned out to be work!

I have baited some places on the river with corn chops from my still—put 'em in a shallow slough off from the river. Once we ran a net there and caught twenty-nine buffalo that weighed 129 pounds in one lick. And we made another set once, up around a little neck in a pond, where we baited it and caught thirty-one buffalo at once. It was customary in those days that a man would own his own boat and trammel nets, but he needed a helper. Like I told you, when I was growing up teenage-like, I would join 'em as a helper on the night's foray. The helper would get one-third of the proceeds, and the man who furnished the boat would get two-thirds. Once we went up Jeems Bayou over in Louisiana to the north of Caddo Lake. Jeems Bayou is a mile-and-a-half wide at its mouth and is a series of small lakes and rivers up through there. We caught 531 pounds of buffalo by four o'clock in the morning. We could have caught.more, but we just couldn't haul 'em. I dressed fish all the way home while the other fellow run the motorboat. We'd get a dime a pound for buffalo, thirteen to fifteen cents for white perch or catfish. We would fish all night and catch a hundred or two hundred pounds of buffalo and make twenty dollars and buy a good deal of stuff.

Course, there was other things to fish for and other methods to fish. There was the spoonbill catfish, the old-time caviar-egg fish. A spoonbill is a long, slender fish that weighed from ten to forty pounds. It looked like a marlin, had kind of a forked tail and slender. It doesn't have any scales, but its hide is pretty tough. It has a paddle for an upper jaw that extends out for one-fourth as long as the rest of its body. Its mouth is down under there, and when it would graze or feed it would turn upside down and skim along the top of the water, picking up plankton or something. It fed like a whale.

Once upon a time, when you looked up and down the river in the summertime, they'd be some days when you could almost continually see a spoonbill jumping in the air. He would jump up about four feet high and fall back. That went on, and Papa would say,

"When the spoonbill are jumping the white perch will bite." He and
I would fish on the river for white perch some in the summer before I
was old enough to branch out in partnership with my uncle. Anyhow, there began to be a demand for the spoonbill eggs, but there was
only one or two who fooled with it. There was a deaf-and-dumb man
down at Taylor Island named Albright who specialized in shipping
fish eggs to New York. Then later in 1921–1922, spoonbill meat got
in demand and would bring two bits a pound in New York. We would
ship it iced down, and we did quite a bit of spoonbill gill net fishing
in them days. We picked up quite a few dollars out of the meat deal.
Then it seemed like the demand for 'em kind of dwindled, and also
the supply. To catch a spoonbill on Caddo Lake today would be an
event. Originally, you would only fish for 'em in February and just
get the egg and throw the fish away. Then there was a little spurt of
demand for the fish themselves, then that died off, and the world
goes on.

There were other ways to fish than gill nets and trammel and hoop
nets. In the days soon after the pearl-hunting days, Caddo Lake had a
lot of buffalo carp in it, and there was this old colored man, a half
Indian, named Foster, who would gig fish in the daytime. He'd shove
around there in shallow water and see a bubble coming up and gig
just behind where it was coming up and hit the fish. Over on Jeems
Bayou side, it was not unusual if you wanted a buffalo for dinner to
wade out in some of those shallow waters and gig him with a gig on
the end of a pole.

I've never done it myself, but some people evolved a system of taking the shot out of a shotgun shell, and maybe part of the powder,
and putting a stick in this shotgun and shooting this stick through
the fish. They'd see the fish maybe four or five feet under the water,
and shoot the stick into him and get him. Also, I've heard people
talking that you could take a handsaw, a carpenter's saw, and hit him
with it down through the water. Chop him in the back, and kill him
and get him.

I gigged fish at night quite a bit back yonder. I used an eight-foot
staff with a good-sized heavy gig on it. The one I've still got was
made out of a pitchfork. A blacksmith had taken this pitchfork and
heated it and hammered it out and changed the direction of the teeth
on it a little, then built beards, you could call it, on the end of it,
where you could stick it in something and it wouldn't come out easy.

You had to have 'em pretty heavy. A big seven- or eight-pound carp,
you'd jab it in around back along his gills area, or in his stomach,
he'd throw a pretty good size fit and could break your handle off.
Some people gigged with a gig on a handle, but with a strong cord

tied to the gig and tied up to the staff. It would come off when it hit the fish. He'd jerk it off, and after he had had his fit and all, they'd stick it back on the pole. That was the method they harpooned whales, you know.

I'd have a flashlight in one hand and the gig in the other, or a fog headlight on. You can see the form of a fish at night in the water even when the water isn't so clear. You can see it down under a ways. I would usually wade around the edge of the bank or the shallow islands out in the lake with a sandy bottom around 'em. You'd wade along the edge of that little timber and find fish piddling around there. Usually, if there's one or two, you'll see more. One year we had an exceptionally good gigging season because the water was kind of low in the late summer and a lot of the open area was shallow. I'd gig a little nearly every night—get a fish or two and a catfish now and then. Got a twenty-two-pound catfish one night.

Then the Galbraiths evolved another fishing system and never told anybody about it except me out of their immediate family. In June a catfish spawns or lays eggs, and they'll get in a hollow stump. There used to be a lot of hollow stumps in the lake that are now rotted off and under the water. The Galbraiths would use a staff about an inch-and-a-half thick by two inches edgeways and ten or twelve feet long. They had a method whereby you could take a big catfish hook and on one side of the staff hollow out a little inset where the hook could set down in the wood. Then you'd notch two nails with the heads cut off and drive 'em into each side of the hook, and it would clip in there and be a pretty rigid contraption. But it would come out under these circumstances. You would tie a string then in the eye of the hook and wrap it around the staff on up there a couple of feet and tie it rigid. You'd stick this down in a hollow stump and the catfish would fight it. He wouldn't run—wouldn't leave the stump from his nest. And you'd work that hook up directly and jerk it and hook him in the belly or somewhere—head, neck, belly, tail, or what. And when he flounced or rolled it'd jerk this hook out of the staff and then he'd be on the line and you could pull him out and get him.

I never caught but a few that way, but I did catch some. You'd get whatever was in there; they'd be eight- or ten-pounders, maybe. These were in stumps that stuck up above the water that were hollow on down below, some of them old big cypress stumps that were hollow. Until a few years ago there were several trees still standing over on the north shore that had a hole cut in 'em. Well, the Galbraiths cut that hole in order to reach down through the hole to see if there was a catfish in there that entered down in a hole below. They'd catch some that way.

One day they caught one over there close to the south shore and took him home across the lake about three miles and put him in the box. Someway or another the old box was ragged and fell apart and the catfish got away. But they went back to that same stump in a day or two and got him again, the scars still in him where they hooked him! They knowed where he was at.

They didn't have any word for this kind of fishing that I heard of, though in South Texas and in some other places there's something they call "coonin'." In the spring catfish will come up there and go along and get under little ledges on the bank. People will go along and feel back in there, and get 'em. They call it "coonin'." You know, like a raccoon does? But the State Game, Fish and Oyster Commission made it against the law. It destroys their nesting grounds, which the Galbraiths done in a way on Caddo Lake by grabbling or cooning them out of the hollow stumps with that pole with a hook on it.

Nets were unlawful, but the sale of the fish was lawful; then in about 1923 the state legislature passed the law prohibiting the sale of game fish, which included bass, white perch, and that's about all. You could still sell catfish and buffalo carp and most anything but the white perch. I had a new T-Model Ford in 1923, and when the railroad quit accepting fish for shipment, the Hartzos and myself made four or five trips to Dallas, hauling T-Model loads of fish up there with ice on 'em. Old man Taylor would sponsor the trip. He would book the fish to these places he had been selling to for years and we would transport them. And that would be an event! Once, I know we had to go by Greenville since you couldn't get from here to Dallas in a T-Model through the Forney Bottom. It had been under water and impassable. Even out around Wills Point there were places in the road where a man and a farmer had a team down there to pull you through.

Once, Jimmy Hall and I loaded five or six hundred pounds of white perch on the T-Model after fishing all night, and we was in Marshall before the ice house opened, and we poured a bunch of ice on 'em soon as it opened and took off for Dallas. We went by Greenville, and we got up there and had the fish sold by three o'clock, then turned around and come back. I got so tired way on in the night I had to stop and sleep. All the way back to Caddo Lake from Greenville in a T-Model!

In them days Jimmy Hall and I camped in tents. I had an army tent right after World War I, when you could buy surplus army tents. Lots of people in the oil fields got those tents, and they was good ones. They had a pole in the middle and went straight up, wigwam-type.

And if you wanted to be uptown in one of 'em you'd get enough lumber to lay a floor just off the ground, and then you'd wall it up about three feet high. Then you'd stretch the tent and let it come down outside of these planks, and that was your habitation.

Me and Jimmy Hall lived once two winters at least down there just this side of the Louisiana line not far from the Jap's camp. We had an army tent that didn't have any planking around it, but we stole enough cotton bagging at the gin house that we had rugs on our floor. And we had beds and a stove over in one corner, a two-foot box stove. We'd run the smokestack out the side and put a piece of tin around it. It worked pretty good, but I remember when we'd sleep three in the bed, and on a real cold night I'd mostly volunteer to sleep in the middle! Then you'd throw your coats and slickers down over the foot of the bed too. It got pretty cold.

The camp was a place to spend either from Sunday evening to Friday, or from Monday morning to Friday. We'd go to the lake, tar nets, change nets, take up and put out in different places, wash 'em out and patch holes in 'em, and stay pretty busy. A lot of the fishing you did at night, some in the daytime if you had a secluded spot back up in the brakes. We'd fish several hundred dollars of nets, and if a game warden had of cleaned us out it'd been quite a bit of expense. Anyway, we'd use them big old hoop nets and haul fish out of there by the thousands of pounds. Unless you caught four or five hundred pounds you wasn't making money, not with just getting twelve or thirteen cents a pound for 'em. Some of the fishermen would sell the catfish and buffalo separate at about twelve cents. Then the game fish, bass and white perch, would bring three or four cents a pound more than the rough fish. And some would make a deal just to throw 'em all together in one price kind of medium-in-between. Them that done that would get a trammel net one night and and catch a bunch of buffalo to throw in with 'em!

Well, that was on the transition from the time when you could sell fish and ship 'em to the time you couldn't. We was still bringing 'em in on the pretext that we was getting 'em in Louisiana. That was another of the complications of Caddo Lake, that it lay in so many counties and states. Fact is, there was nearly always some quandary going on about what the law was, or wasn't. The fact that Caddo Lake lay in Marion County and Harrison County and Caddo Parish, and in Texas and Louisiana, made things kinda complicated for law enforcement officers. If the grand jury was meeting in Marshall and we was afraid they was going to summon somebody, we might go over and spend the night with the Galbraiths or the Jap in the other county.

Or if it got too hot in Texas, it wasn't too far to the Louisiana line.

Once, when Jim Casey was county attorney in Marshall, the fishermen got together and decided that we'd make a test case out of bringing fish from Louisiana and see if it wasn't legal to do it. They elected me to be the guinea pig, says, "You ain't married, and if you do get in jail it won't be like us other people." Anyway, I went down early one morning and caught fifteen or twenty pounds of fish and brought 'em on up to Dr. Lankford, the game warden. He knew about the episode, seemingly, and brought me on to town, just very agreeable, but the prosecuting attorney wouldn't file charges. He called Austin and they didn't know what to do. But they knew what to do pretty soon, because they amended the law to say you can't sell white perch from Louisiana in Texas!

One time there was another argument ensued here about laws. The law read "Caddo Lake and its tributaries." Well, we saw a loophole there when we found that tributaries wasn't mentioned in the law that closed the season in March and April, so we proceeded to fish in the river. The argument was, "Where does the tributary quit being and where does the lake start?" The argument was over when they done amended that law and put tributaries back in it.

A county commissioner told me once, Mr. Joe Bibb, he said, "It's not as bad for a native of the lake like you are to try to make a living off it as it was for some sportsman to come down and violate the laws who wasn't as broke as you was." Of course, in them days we felt that the laws was an infringement on our Indian rights to fish anywhere we wanted to. The first game wardens were about 1914 or 1915, somewhere around there. Up until then there were some sort of fish laws, but they were just on the books and not much enforced. Nobody had motorboats, and when you got down on Big Lake it was a long way from habitation, and pulling boats with oars didn't appeal to the game warden too much. I've jokingly told the present warden that when the state hired the first four game wardens, they put one on the coast, one in West Texas, and two on Caddo Lake. Caddo was the only lake then; there wasn't none of these lakes northwest and west of here. From here to El Paso was dry! And when you said, Let's go to the lake," you was talking about Caddo.

The early game wardens . . . there was a Cunningham, kind of a tall, slender fellow. I can remember him vaguely. There was a Goodfellow, sort of a chunky fellow, and at that time they established what they called the "Statehouse" on the lake adjacent to a fellow named Joe Dixon. Joe was a duck hunter and fisherman and outlaw, but he got along pretty good with Goodfellow. In fact, Goodfellow would come over towards Joe's house and visit there while he was gone. One day Joe come in a little earlier than he ought to and old Goodfellow kind of hurriedly left the house. While he was crawling through the fence, Dixon popped him with duckshot. That stopped him from prowling over there. Then there was a Bun Rowe, who was an uncle to Judge Rowe. They worked together somewhat. Bun Rowe was there along in the mid-teens and was kind of a gangster sort. If you talked to him just right, furnished him with some drinking material . . . to tell you the truth, he had kind of a deal with old man Taylor for a little rake-off per pound of fish that was sold. That's the only rake-off I ever heard of. I hate to bring that up, but since it happened I did. Later, Bun Rowe was over on the north shore on a drinking spree one day at the Jap's camp, which at that time was a tent that had been left by an oil drilling company. A fellow, Griffis, was over there, and he and Bun Rowe got in an argument or something, and Griffis went home and got a gun and come back and shot Bun Rowe in the head. They held a trial in Jefferson and the Jap was the only witness. He shook his head and grunted and claimed that he couldn't understand a word of English, which he could, and wound up with no conviction. They called it self-defense. Then there was an Albert Hall, who was a pretty rough old man who believed in force and carried two big guns. He was mean. He was mean enough that later on he got mad at a fellow and killed him in the city hall in Marshall. Doc Lankford, the one that I allowed myself to be arrested by, was a gentlemanly old man who tried to educate people from the bank on the value of conservation. He sold lots of fishing and hunting licenses.

I was thinking about something that happened sixty or seventy years ago. Back in the teens, when I camped on Caddo Lake at Swanson's Landing with my uncle and fished nets on halves, we didn't have a motor. Did all of our work by oarlocks in a pulling wooden skiff. There was an old colored man named John Davis who would come down to the camp and help clean up around and eat with us and stuff. After we'd eat, he'd eat syrup and biscuits and bacon. Uncle John was a fixture around there for years. Then in the thirties, when I moved to the lake down there and started making whiskey and shooting ducks and building boats and duck blinds and working in the oil fields and digging a living out of the lake, Uncle John had done got old and lived up in the country.

But he'd show up now and then to visit with me a little bit. And the old rascal had an old wooden boat down the bank, and was nearly always stuck out there in the lake fishing for brim and pestering me. Maybe he might have helped me fish my illegal fishing nets sometimes. We was making whiskey down the bank, and one day me and Crip Haddock was coming back up the bank and there set Uncle John's boat. We got to looking at it, and the cracks in it was an inch wide and he had almost a bale of cotton in them cracks to keep that old craft floating. We decided in a fit of anger that old man John Davis didn't belong on the lake no more nohow, and that we'd just eliminate him as being a potential hazard. We had an axe in the boat and we hit the side of his boat a big lick back toward the back end and knocked a whole chunk out of it right down close to the bottom.

Well, we felt bad when we sobered up, I imagine, but didn't do anything about it. A few days later I was out there, and I looked over and setting right in front of where my still was in a gap was a kind of peculiar-looking craft. I went over there, and it was Uncle John Davis setting up on the bow end of his boat afishing. He was setting so that hole cocked up out of the water where it wouldn't leak! And there he went. I thought to myself I ought to build him a new boat. Now he was a man who rose to the occasion. If it leaked in the back end he rode the front end, or vice versa.

I still fish my nets, even now. I got oodles of gill net. It don't matter much where you put it out; them buffalo will prowl. The main problem now is you can't hardly find open water. There's moss or lilies or something there. An ideal place to put it is to cut a road through some lilies with your motor and then put it up and down that opening. Up and down it is the only place you can put it if you want it to sink.

Way I put 'em out, I take a piece of three-inch gill net, the lawful size, about a hundred feet long, about as long as I have it. I go down there on Big Lake where them islands are, and it ain't over waist deep, and find a spot and put on my wading pants and just wade through there and put it out. Then sprinkle some corn chops over it. You'll catch some. You put it out in wading water, up in timber where boats wouldn't run, in those little thick trees. Just put out a piece that, when you stretch it on top of the water, you won't have to have no floats, no weights, or nothing.

I got some sets down there now. Wade up in the islands and stretch it out—run it out with a bucket. If it's long enough and wants to sag in the middle, I'll just tap a nail in a tree and hang it over. Then you sprinkle chops down it. I just put some chops in the bottom of the bucket with the net on top of it. Just go down there and run up to one of these points and get out and wade up there. That way a boat won't hit you. You can't put it out where there's current to do no good, it'll wrap up. And you can't put it out in the open lake because if it comes a wind, it'll roll up like a rope. But down this north shore there's some islands in there that are thick enough that you can work a boat up to it. And maybe there ain't no moss there either. Oh, there's plenty of places to put out a gill net!

Of course, fishing or hunting on Caddo Lake could be dangerous. Every once and a while they'd be a drowning. My Uncle George Bonner, my friends Edward and Aubry Hartzo, and my double-first cousin Crip Haddock all died on the lake.

One Sunday they called me and said there had been two drownings. I went down and learned a little about it. One man had been recovered, and they had him on the bank trying to revive him, but they failed. I went down and found the other man at the end of his own trotline. They were fishing a trotline in what we called the river, but it's down in the area where there's lake all alongside. They had thrown a rock overboard that looked like it weighed fifty pounds. I don't know why the fellows needed that much rock. But the rock got hung on something and a fisherman boat off a ways heard them hollering. This man was actually hooked on his own trotline. I picked him up and went to the funeral home the next day.

The Hartzos drowned in '44, the two brothers and a Hadlock from Marshall. Apparently they were out in front of Swanson's Landing, two of 'em in a duck blind, Edward Hartzo and this Hadlock, and Aubry Hartzo had carried the boat off to another blind. That night I was at work in the plant when we got the word that they hadn't shown up. There'd been quite a norther that evening about three o'clock, because there was a black cloud whipped up out of the north and blew pretty stiff as I was going to work.

Well, the next morning they still hadn't showed up, so I went to the lake soon as possible. It had turned extremely cold then. Charlie Hale and I went down through the lake and we begin to discover wreckage down there in Big Lake, like decoy ducks hung up on stumps. And we found floating debris, probably out of the boat, over on the Swanson's shore—oars, gas cans, peanut butter jars partly eaten, and maybe a cushion or something. As we proceeded up the bank, we found the boat turned upside down with the motor still on it. Then we were able to about pinpoint the blind they were in, Edward Hartzo and this Hadlock, and in another blind there were cigarettes that were characteristic of the way Aubry Hartzo rolled Bull Durham. We surmised that Aubry had been in the blind with the boat, and when the storm hit he went over and they started trying to take up stuff and didn't make it. We found a coat not far from the blind, and about a hundred yards from the blind we found Mr. Hadlock. But the wind had changed its course as it developed, and as you got further from the blind the area of possibly finding somebody got wider, so we weren't able to find the other two bodies till they came up about ten days later.

Then in 1924, a friend of mine, Mr. Jimmy Hall, and I were fishing in the summer on Caddo Lake—had a few trotlines out and some gill nets. My Uncle George Bonner, who was in his forties then, went with us down the north shore to the Jap's place. We visited a while there and then went out across the lake. It was on June 8 and nice weather, no particular wind. We started taking up a string of gill nets out in Big Lake in front of Swanson's Landing. We had caught several large buffalo carp and some spoonbill cat and gar and stuff, and had the boat pretty well filled with fish. The old motor on it was one of them old time Evinrudes that weighed 110 pounds.

Anyway, a little breeze came up about noon like it does lots of times. In the course of taking the nets up, one of 'em hung on a stump, and in pulling it in I was pulling the boat down a little bit. And there was a bad place on the boat where nets had been pulled in and had worn a place next to a rib, and there was a nail sticking up there, and this gill net hung on it, and before I got it off the thing sunk! We were all there in the water together with fish swimming around us in the net. Then the back end of the boat went down and it turned over. The bow continued to stay up but was slick on top. My uncle washed away from it. I got my rubber boots off and was able to swim to a stump. Mr. Hall, he caught ahold of a wood seat that helped him float, and he found a stump a good ways from me. But Uncle George didn't make it. He apparently became terribly scared and went down and never did come up. We stayed there from when our watch had stopped at twelve-thirty till about seven o'clock, which was getting along toward sundown. We hollered and considered trying to swim to the bank or trying to swim over to a pipeline, which had a telephone line on it, to see if we could maybe tear it down or someway get somebody to come. Then, just before dark, Mr. Harvey came along with his brother pulling a skiff, and we stood up and managed to attract their attention and they brought us home. Then we immediately begin to try to go back and search for Uncle George. The Johnson Brothers Ranch rigged us up a boat. It was dark, but by ten o'clock we were able to find him. He had almost undressed. Apparently after he sank he attempted to pull his clothes off. But I had been watching close; when he went down he didn't come up.

That was the only drowning I was ever actually at, but I've helped hunt for a good many that did drown. Some of 'em was old fishermen, that, as one fellow expressed it, "had been on the lake all their lives, and could swim, and never had got drowned before."

VI

During the "teens," when I was camping on the lake with my uncle, the Gulf Oil Company were beginning the heyday of offshore drilling. Offshore drilling was born right there with Gulf Oil Company on Caddo Lake, the first offshore drilling that's known. There was a little offshore drilling in California, but it was done by building a platform out to a well a slight distance from the bank. Here at Caddo they used tugboats and barges and pile drivers and drove pilings. Cutting piling up at Uncertain in the wooded area of Caddo Lake was quite an industry there.

Caddo Lake hadn't always been Caddo Lake. I have a Corps of Engineers report from the 1870's that calls it "Fairy Lake." And then when Gulf Oil come, and there was offshore drilling in the lower lake, the lease from the Louisiana Levee Board lists their wells down there not in Fairy but in "Ferry Lake." The wells were listed Ferry Lake #4, Ferry Lake #5, and so forth.

After the wells had been drilled a good deal, in the early twenties, there was one drilled that hit a pocket of oil and blew out. I was camping over at the Jap's camp at that time, another fellow and I. I had a little box camera and went down there and taken pictures of that six-inch stream of oil coming out of the ground and splattering over the top of a hundred-foot wooden derrick, and the south wind blowing a stream of pure oil towards the bank a half-mile away. If that had caught afire down there, that would have been a calamity. I had some of the Gulf Oil workmen tell me that the oil had gotten so thick, blowing from this Ferry Lake #215, that when they drove a motorboat through it, it was thick enough on the water that it made the boat float up high enough that the propeller would spin! So you know it was pretty deep. That was some kind of pollution, but nobody would worry, in fact said it "looked pretty."

Like I told you, when the Gulf Oil Company was on their drilling boom in Caddo Lake and was drilling offshore, they were acquiring the pilings of logs to drive in the ground to make the foundations for their rigs. They would require 108 pilings for each rig. These were cypress trees a foot-and-a-half big at the big end and tapered down to eight or ten inches at the little end, and maybe twenty-five or thirty feet long. That was around 1914, because I helped with pulling them to Mooringsport. I was sort of the deckhand on the boat. The log-cutters lived here at Karnack; a family named Moore were timber workers, but not related to me. They cut all around on Eagle's Nest and a lot of the area there. They would drag the logs to the river and put 'em in rafts of about eight or ten logs wide, then wire 'em together and nail some timbers across 'em to hold. Then they'd tie that raft to another until they had 108 pilings in the string. It would probably be four or five hundred feet long, all told. There was a man at Uncertain who had a contract for delivering them down to the place on Caddo Lake where they wanted 'em. He had rented an old tugboat thing from Mooringsport. I would join him, and when we hooked onto a raft up in Alligator Bayou in the river, I'd get back on the raft with a prod pole and help it around the corners. Then, when we got on down to the ditches and open lake, I'd get in the main boat. It would move awful slow. They would have a predestined location further down there in Big Lake where they was going to take the Gulf Oil Company pile drive and drive those pilings. They had a blueprint to go by—so many for the main derrick foundation, then some off to the side for a mud tank to sit on, then some to stack for a platform to put their pipes on. Then they'd have a long walk-way on off two or three hundred feet and another platform out there to set a boiler on. That was to lessen the danger of fire. There's some of the old derrick locations still down there.

A little after that time, my Aunt Jennie moved with her husband, Stanley Hayner, who used to work on the snag boat, down in Louisiana. They were working in the oil field down there. I was about seventeen then, or maybe a little older, and I began to go off to Aunt Jennie's down at Goss, Louisiana, and work in the oil fields. I was helping clear new ground down there to drill wells when I was pretty young. They used to figure you had to be twenty-one years old to work, but the saying was, that if they asked you how old you was, tell 'em you'd had the seven years' itch three times and it'd started on you again!

So I did quite a little bit of oil field work down there, and finally, around 1920, Papa decided he'd go to work in the oil fields. Well, he was too old, I was most too young, but he was more too old to go than I was too young.

Anyway, we hooked up and sold our cows at home, turned the mules aloose in the pasture, and Papa got Mr. Taylor and Wade Futrell to move us down there in his big old trailer truck. Papa had a job already promised and we moved out in the woods and camped in a tent. Papa fired a boiler station and I worked on a lease over there as a roustabout. Then I drifted off over toward Red River and spent a winter over there. Buddy, my brother, never would stay down there much. He'd stay at home. He raised the crops the year we was gone and probably come out better than we did. Finally, we moved back and started over again.

The first oil field was discovered on the banks of Caddo Lake in Oil City, Louisiana, around 1904, not long after Spindletop. The Gulf Oil Company leased the lake bed, but they didn't begin to drill it until after the first dam was built. Before the dam was built, I think there were some platforms run out from the bank, and they would drill the edges of the lake, just slightly offshore. Then when the dam was built, Gulf Oil Company established quite a landing at Mooringsport, with a warehouse and hoists and stuff to unload barges. And they had a pretty good bunch of wooden barges, eighteen by fifty feet long. They'd haul the little steam-drilling rig out there and slide it up a slide onto the platform where it was sitting on the 108 pilings, and a wooden derrick would be put up, and they'd proceed to drill. The pumping rig in those days was quite a big outfit—the old big flywheel engine that would weigh several thousand pounds. They took it out there in pieces, probably, and assembled them. There was a "big bend wheel" and "bull wheels" and "walking beams" and all that old-time stuff. It was quite a deal, but the wells were only two-thousand-something feet deep, which is shallow. But they had elaborate pump equipment in those days, and there were hundreds of 'em out there. Steel derricks didn't come along until well in the twenties.

Like I told you, my first oil field work was around 1917, over in what was called the Bull Bayou Field. We'd clear places to drill wells. We'd saw down trees and drag the logs and burn 'em, and clean off a not-so-big place them days. By about 1918 I worked on a drilling rig awhile, then I was back up here on a wildcat with the same driller I'd worked for down there. I was hired to fire the boiler with cordwood.

Those days, you just hired to the driller. There was a company, but they didn't particularly check your health, and there wasn't any insurance. It was up in the twenties before I ever remember them sending you to a doctor before they hired you. The driller just hired you and would run you off in the middle of the shift if he didn't like the way you done. You was completely subservient to the driller.

It was like going out there twelve hours a day and working! Five people would work the rigs. It would be a boiler fireman and a derrick man and a driller and two helpers. The helpers would help the boiler fireman fire the boiler with wood. The derrick man was supposed to run the rig some if the driller wasn't there, or while the driller rested a little. But the derrick man usually oiled the machinery and would take the pumps apart and put packing in 'em. He'd be

Vernon and Wyatt Moore, Karnack, Texas, 1907.

Wyatt (right) and younger brother, Walter Lewis Moore, 1945.

Wyatt and Jimmy Hall at their fishing camp on Lake Caddo about 1918.

*Wyatt's custom-built 1919 Model T carried one 10-gallon
and two 5-gallon jugs of moonshine.*

Wyatt's camp house during 1930 Caddo flood.

*Galbraith-built inboard boat on Wyatt's improvised dry dock,
about 1934.*

Complete standard wood oil rig, mid-1930's.

Wyatt on Lake Caddo, 1970.

Moore's TUSH HOG pulls government barge, 1974. Wyatt and U.S. engineers worked Big Cypress to the dam and back again before money ran out.

Fiftieth anniversary of Ona Belle and Wyatt, May 4, 1975.

Ona Belle and Wyatt, 1924.

Moore works on a skiff in his backyard, 1976. In the background (left) is a finished bateau.

Wyatt proudly holds a model he made of a Galbraith boat, 1976.

using one of the helpers. Then everybody fell in when they put up pipe or pulled out of the hole. The boiler fireman couldn't spend too much time on the floor, but he'd spend some.

You dug the pits with a shovel where they now bulldoze 'em. You set the rig up in pieces. It would come from posts to bolt to the derrick, then you would lift by some sort of an improvised rope-and-chain "tom hoist" and lift the drive shaft and line shaft up there. Then you'd put the drum in there and put the chains on. While they were moving, they would put these chains in a tub or pot and boil 'em in a heavy oil they thought would preserve 'em. But it didn't, it was too thick. Then you'd set the boiler up there, and in the oil fields you'd fire with gas, usually. In the woods around Caddo you'd burn wood. I've worked on five or six T. J. Taylor Number One Wildcats, and I fired the boilers all with wood. I got to be pretty well known around as a good wood fireman, which isn't much to brag on now but was then. It was hard work. I'd wear a heavy wool shirt so the boiler heat wouldn't blister me.

Mr. Taylor was just leasing the land. Some promoter would get a big block of land and sell enough prospective frontage to people that wanted to take the chance to see if he got a well, and would state the contract depth they were going to go. Mostly, when we drilled the wells, we wollered it down to that contract depth, and a justice of the peace or a local surveyor, or somebody, would bring a notary public out and watch us pull the pipe out of the ground and measure to prove the contractor had fulfilled his promises. That would be the end of it. About the only way you could discover oil would be it would blow out on you. You didn't particularly look for tests. It was left up to the driller to see if he thought he went through any oil. We'd watch the mud pits to see if some oil would come out—watch if there was any gas bubbles. Most of the native citizenry around would come watch. They'd see oil on the pit which fell off the drilling rig and claim there was oil there, but we'd pump the well full of mud and leave it.

They never had a fire out on the lake that I can recall, but they had some fires on the bank. One of the fires on the bank was caused from the well blowing out and creating a kind of crater. It didn't have any casing in to control it then, and it caught on fire. One well over there burned for a year or more. There wasn't any attempt being made to put it out; it just finally quit of its own accord. There were hoboes that would come there and camp at night, and people fishing on the lake would set up camp around there way off in the back in order to have heat. That was around 1907. You could see it burning from here in Karnack. I don't remember ever going to it, but some people went over to it with "chug-chug" motorboats. My friend Franklin Jones of Marshall went with a party over there, and a Mr. Warren knocked a hole in the boat somewhere on the way over and give up and went to hollering, "We're all goin' to drown!" But some fellow managed to stick a shirt in the hole and get the boat bailed out and save it till they got to the bank. Then they nailed a board over it and come home.

I never was on a wildcat that blew out around here, but in the field I've been on a couple of blowouts and went to some wells down below Bull Bayou to help stop a blowout. The well would be blowing and they'd manage to run drill pipe in it and mix up a whole bunch of mud, chimbley-looking mud, gumbo mud from somewhere, and we'd try to pump it in there to get the pipe filled up with mud and get it stopped. You'd take a big joint of pipe and screw it on above the valve and fill that big joint of pipe full of mud. Then you would close the top of it and open the valve and let that mud fall in the well. Then you'd close the valve again and fill that big pipe full of mud again. Finally, you got the well full of heavy mud heavier than the gas pressure was, you hoped, and the blowout would stop.

People talk about pollution nowadays, but they ought to have been here then! I told you about that day I observed oil blowing out of Ferry Lake #215 over the top of the wooden derrick. It was along into the spring, and the wind was from the south, and a stream of oil was falling for a half-mile from the rig. This well blew out maybe the rest of that day or maybe into the next day. I don't know when they cut it off. Apparently they didn't lose control of it, but was just letting it blow.

It was just customary then to let them "clean themselves," they called it—to blow out for a day, or maybe two. They had a valve on the well, and when it blew out, they loosened the drill pipe, pulled it up, loosened it off the bottom. Then they stuck it back in the hole and unscrewed from it, then closed the valve. This was actually detrimental to the well, because the oil and gas rumbling down in the bottom and flowing wide open would create a lessening of pressure, and the salt water below it would come up and mix with the oil sand. Nowadays they think that vast areas of oil are in little traps of it down there where the wells were allowed to flow too freely.

Nobody ever thought anything about pollution—no idea about it, apparently. There was oil slicks nearly every which-a-where around them days. They'd be a slick of oil come up from down in Louisiana and blow up in Texas and finally wind up on the bank. The wind would bring it in. They'd be signs of oil around trees, and it would finally coagulate and disappear. Some places where it was thick enough, they'd get a fire out there and it would burn up some trees and leave a naked-looking place. Finally, more trees would grow up.

Pollution that way these days, people would think was the end of the world, and it might would be. Up Jeems Bayou, which is the tributary to the north of the lake, there was drilling going on in the lake and on the bank. A lot of the wells would make salt water— Tiger Creek up there was running in the lake almost pure salt water— and these salt-water flows would kill the timber. It didn't particularly bother the fish, apparently. Some fish are semi-salt-water-like, you know, and some of the carp-like fish up Jeems Bayou hung around some of those creeks that salt water was flowing in, and maybe even went up 'em some. Fish have a tendency to come to where ever there's fresh water flowing in. The fish seemed to be in good condition, but their fins and tails would be eaten down pretty knubby-like. People could tell if they was Jeems Bayou–caught fish, or not. But we'd catch carp and buffalo by the hundreds of pounds. One night, Edward Hartzo and I with one trammel net caught 513 pounds—all we thought Mr. Taylor could sell and about all the boat could hold safely.

Of course the biggest pollution that ever killed fish that I saw was from the war plant in Karnack, which was dumping waste water from washing TNT powder. It was letting go into Goose Prairie, which was a three- or four-hundred-acre lake tributary there, and it turned that water red-looking and killed off every kind of life. There wasn't a tadpole or a minnow or a frog or anything in it for two or three years. And it killed fish on down as far as midway in the lake. In 1944, when the Hartzos drowned and we were dragging for 'em down there in December, there was dead fish just everywhere you looked. But it didn't affect all the lake, and when the pollution quit being put in and fresh water come and all, it recovered.

Nowdays I'm amused that Shreveport's waterworks is wanting to get water out of Caddo Lake. Their excuse is that Cross Lake, which is the alternative water source, would be dangerous to build a highway bridge across because they might drive piling into an old well that was drilled there several years ago and pollute the lake. Then, the lake might get polluted by a wreck on the bridge—if they ever built it. And the railroad out there, which isn't across the lake, just across the dam, might pollute the lake. So they want water out of Caddo Lake instead, and Caddo Lake already has two railroads and five highway bridges and a thousand old half-drilled wells in it, and the biggest chemical plant in the South sitting on the bank of it! They're not afraid of that pollution.

Charlie Casey's name is over there in the Oil Field Museum at Kilgore. They quote Charlie Casey of Mount Enterprise as saying things about the good old oil field days when they worked twelve hours a day seven days a week, and if they got a blowout or something, sometimes they'd work thirty hours without quitting.

I knew Charlie Casey as early as 1919 or so down on Bull Bayou, the Mansfield, Louisiana, area, out there right where the hills go off into the Red River Valley. Charlie Casey was just out of the World War. He'd been a motorcycle rider in the army, and had rode motorcycle in France carrying messages. If they had an important message to send they would dispatch three motorcycles, so maybe one of 'em would get there. Charlie was a rather large Irishman, dark-complected, swarthy, and had a big chew of tobacco way out in his jaw a lot of the time. He was the transportation man for the Clark and Greer Drilling and Production Company that we were working for. He drove a Caterpillar tractor and pulled an eight-wheeled wagon to haul oil field equipment to and from the rig. I was working on the roustabout gang, but sometimes I'd work on the rig some if they got in a tight.

They had a blacksmith shop there on the lease, and a boarding house and quite a place. My mother and dad had moved down there and I was camping over there with 'em and working on the lease. Anyway, we all admired Charlie Casey. They had a little smart-alec man there running the boarding house, him and his wife, and he also had a buggy with two horses that he kept up for the tool pusher to go when the roads was too bad for even a T-Model. One day this boy brought in two nice leather straps from town to go from the axle on the buggy on up to the doubletree. Me and Charlie seed 'em laying there in the barn and we tried 'em on and they made us a good belt. They was about an inch wide and just fit. So I carried mine home and laid it up, but Charlie kept wearing his. Day or two later, this fellow missed 'em and he got to raising cain about what he'd do to whoever stole 'em. Charlie listened at him a while and finally he pooched his belly out and says, "Does that look like one of 'em?" Fellow says, "I believe it does." Charlie says, "Well, go ahead and get it if you can." So then I started wearing mine too!

After those days, Charlie drifted over to Mount Enterprise, Texas, and married, and I'd visit with him down through the years on my way down to Lufkin and back. He had a feed store over there and also maintained a service for water wells.

Back here in the transition days, when the civil rights movement was gaining big momentum, they was having an election down there at Mount Enterprise, and there was a little fidgety colored man come up there a day or two before the election. Charlie was election judge, and he had an imposing appearance. If he said something was that way, it was like an umpire in a ball game, it was that way! But this little colored man kind of fidgets, says, "Mr. Casey, I hears us colored folks gonna vote dis time uptown in de election Saturday." "Well, yeah," Casey says, "I understand some of you gonna vote, but there's one little hitch in it." Says, "The first one comes, we gonna kill him and lay him across the door and the rest of y'all can just step over him and come on in." I don't know what the outcome of that 'lection was, but that was about like Charlie to tell 'em that, and maybe stick to it.

One time there was a man come in this country who was a sure-enough oil and water witcher. He was an oil man and did drill some wells, and had studied water witching and oil witching. He had several boxes with different kinds of "doodlebugs," we called 'em. He drilled a well out here right east of Karnack about a mile, and I helped him some—fired the boilers a few days.

Well, he used to visit with me down at the lake. One day I was drilling out there on a water well and was gone, but when I come in he said, "Moore, you're wasting your time out there on that water well. Ain't no water there." Well, he had his doodlebugs and believed in 'em, and sure enough I didn't get water. But he had doodlebugged on down south of the house, and he says, "There's a little sign of some water down that way." And years later I drilled a well down there and did get a little water. Anyway, one day I carried him out on the lake to doodlebug for oil in the boat. And he doodlebugged around there, and he'd say "go over this way" or "go back over this way," and he'd watch them doodlebugs and scratch his head. Finally, I went right over the Gulf Pipe Line. "Man," he says, "this is a good spot!" I says, "Hell yes, there's a pipe line right there under the water." But I guess that damn thing must have told him something.

VII

Along in the twenties I bought Mr. Drayton Powell's old T-Model from the Hawley Motor Company for sixty-five dollars, and that was my first car. In those days them T-Models had a gravity-flow gas tank, and up a steep hill the gas wouldn't flow out of the tank to the carburetor, so you'd have to turn around and back up 'em. I got it home, but I had to back up Eight-Mile Hill! Crip Haddock, my crippled first cousin, was staying with us then, and we got the bed off of it. It didn't have any battery on it, no starter on it. You cranked it by hand, and you had magneto lights. Anyway, we got the body off it and was gonna build what we called a "racer," with a homemade body on it, but we couldn't stand to wait. Crip got on the back of the frame and I got on the gas tank, and we drove off down the Big Road.

In those days the roads consisted of an opening through the woods with some deep ruts in 'em, usually. After it hadn't rained for a few days you could get up between the ruts and travel. We was able to keep this T-Model between the ruts for a while, but we got down the road there about a half-a-mile and something went a little wrong and we run over and fell in the ruts. When it did, it threw me off, and I fell over between the wheels on my stomach and the hind wheels run over me, run over my legs. But there wasn't no weight there, hardly; it didn't hurt me. I jumped up to try to catch it, but Crip had managed to crawl up there and push the gas lever up and it sorta turned out and run into Mr. Baker's fence and stopped.

Anyway, we got that vehicle builded and I ran that thing several years, and did lots of hauling of drinking material in it. We already knew that Prohibition had come, but about that time a lot of people decided they couldn't put up with Prohibition no longer!

It had begun to be a little experimental moonshining around. Prohibition came in 1918, but that didn't mean you couldn't get something to drink for a year or two afterwards. Louisiana was somehow or other a little slower about getting dry than Texas, and we would motorboat down to Mooringsport and pick up stuff. Older people would order liquor—you could order a gallon per person—and they'd take three or four of us pretty-good-size teenage boys down there to claim our gallon. I know one day Joe Dixon gave me the name of J. E. Norman, and I rared back and walked up to the depot counter in Louisiana and asked for a package for J. E. Norman. This fellow kind of looked over his glasses at me and says, "Naw, but there's one here for J. A. Norman." Says, "Who is it from?" Well, I could remember the name of a firm in Monroe they called J. E. Block and I named that firm. He laughed and give it to me. He knew how it was, but I didn't know he knew it.

We'd watch on the way back at the state line to see if somebody might be watching for us, and cross the line back into dry Texas. There was some that would order to Greenwood, Louisiana, and go down on the train to pick it up. But they was a little afraid to go on the train, 'cause there wasn't no way to run on a train! In a boat you could turn around or go the other way, go some which-a-how.

So that went on for a while till Prohibition really got started. There was a county judge here in Marshall whose brother was kind of an outlaw like the rest of us. Us and this brother would make moonshine down on the lake and haul it to Marshall. We wasn't too scared because we thought we had a little backup system maybe if we got caught, with this other fellow's brother being the county judge. We would go over in a little shed-room pottery store in North Marshall after we got rid of a load of moonshine and grab us a bunch of jugs out there on the edge of the street. One time we was grabbing a bunch of jugs and we didn't notice 'em close, and when we got home we found they was chicken-watering jugs! You know they're builded with no opening at the top, and they got a cork in the bottom and a little trough built out there? You can fill 'em up, and they'll only feed water out as the chickens need it.

But things went on and I worked in the oil fields and continued to have a little moonshine operations, and got married in 1925. We lived in Waskom with Mrs. Anderson. I worked the oil field around there for two or three years. But in the wintertime I wouldn't work much, I'd go home and prepare for other people's Christmases. I had a pretty good bunch of people that I knew, and I'd fish some and make enough money to maintain me a method of transportation. At that time we didn't have any children. Then about 1926 I went out to Cisco, Texas, with a native Caddo Lake man who was working for the Game, Fish and Oyster Commission, and I spent nearly a year out there fishing in Lake Cisco, catching fish for the hatchery and hauling fish and so forth.

Then my wife and I got on the passenger train and came home. I picked up a little old T-Model and peddled fish that winter, and me and Charley Hale had a winter's vacation with a little moonshining and buffalo fishing and stuff.

I'd fired boilers on five T. J. Taylor wildcats around Karnack, and got to be in demand as a boiler firer, but I wanted to leave the oil field and start something else. So in 1929 I acquired me a couple of acres of ground down on Caddo Lake in the Big Lake area and built me a shotgun-rough house out of green, fresh-cut pine lumber that I got from the Taylor Brothers sawmill here in Marshall. I got in that house and stayed in it for fifteen years, and that fifteen years was when events picked up. Ironically, this old house that I built in 1929 out of rough pine lumber is still standing today with the same sheet-iron roof on it. People are still living in it. So I don't know of anybody that built anything that lasted any longer than that.

But we moved down to the house on the lake around 1930, and I built boats and fished and hunted and sold minnows and had a fishing camp. Didn't have any electric power, but someone gave me a carbide plant that ran with gas and I rigged that up. We had wood-burning stoves there, and it wasn't many years before we acquired a fireplace, and a good one. We cooked on it a whole lot. The two children, Gloria and Martha, were born around 1931 and 1933, and they thought it was a big thing to fry fish on the fireplace and eat on the bench by the light of the fire and throw the bones in the fireplace. In building the fireplace, I established a beam in there that I could swing out and hang a pot on. And we kept a dutch oven affair, that's a big skillet with legs on it you can put fire under and fire on top of and can do real good cooking with. I had cooked for years on ones back in the teens when I camped with my uncles down at Swanson's Landing and fished nets on halves.

In 1929 it came fourteen inches of snow between the time the first snow come and the other melted, and we were completely isolated for three weeks or a month. We had an old T-Model Ford that would run if you'd have poured hot water on the manifold and got it started, but you couldn't leave there in it. The lake froze over. We weren't suffering for groceries. We had several fish in the box, and I'd go down every day and check the lake, and knock a hole in the ice every evening and get a couple of big white perch while my wife was building a fire and putting the cooking utensils on. We'd throw the fish in the skillet while they was still fluttering and really have fresh fish! Every night we'd think we wouldn't want fish again the next day, but seems like they got to tasting good again by the next evening. We didn't have a radio, telephone, TV or nothing, and hardly ever heard an airplane go over. At Mr. Garret's place next door to us, he had a little battery radio, so I'd raise the window on that side and stick my head in and listen at the early morning report on the news from KWKH Shreveport, and get the weather report. I remember when I first heard that Huey P. Long had died from a newscaster by the name of Bob Shipley.

Anyway, I gradually drifted back into the moonshining business. Like I told you, it was a year or so after national Prohibition, the Volstead Act, before you couldn't get a little bit of bonded liquor that people had stored up. My old man liked him a drink now and then, and he had got him a whole barrel. Then people got to fooling with trying to make it on the small scale, using a small copper five- or ten-gallon pot, and some even blowed up the syrup bucket with it! We didn't know much about how to do it at first. I don't know if we ever used any information from old moonshiners back in the East, Kentucky and Virginia and the like, but the news finally got around. Finally a lot of the people was making it, and Harrison County was listed as the "moonshine capital of Texas" right into the 1950's.

In fact, I have a newspaper clipping that says Harrison County is still the moonshine capital of Texas. In the early fifties, one year, there was more stills found in Harrison County than in all the rest of the state combined. That was something. Out of 254 counties, one county surpassed the other 253!

But in the early days, each moonshiner would brag on how he'd found a better way. It finally wound up to where about the standard rig around here was two wooden barrels. You'd get wooden barrels from the Coca-Cola bottling works, or else use bakery-type lard barrels. Them lard barrels would be pretty greasy inside, but you'd build a little fire in 'em, sort of burn the lard out, and then throw water in there. It might char them a little, but they made good mash barrels. Or you could get two oil drums and boil 'em out good with soap and water and get 'em clean. You'd set your barrels or drums up in the woods on the bank of the creek or lake and put in a hundred pounds of corn chops or rye, half in one barrel and half in the other—usually go back in isolated places. Then, maybe, to begin with, you'd put some yeast cake in there and warm the water and a day or so later warm it again. If you ever got it started to working good, you could continue to put more sugar on the old chop. And sometimes, you'd put in new sugar and partly old mash back in your barrels after you'd wrung the whiskey out of it in your cooker, and it would be ready to run again in three or four more days.

That would make somewhere from seven to as much as ten or eleven gallons of moonshine to the hundred pounds of sugar, which was a really good turnout. A lot of people would make one of these "sets," they called it, kind of a hideout down on the creek bottom, and put in a bunch and let it get ready and spend about a day and a night down there running it. Then they'd quit before it'd get found.

By 1920 it was pretty much of an industry. Nearly all the natives made a little down behind the barn at the spring, or had a bigger thing on Caddo Lake. Naturally I joined in with 'em. I didn't think it was a thrill, but them days it was about that or nothing. There wasn't any unemployment or layoffs. Wasn't nobody working in the first place! It got to be a pretty good industry—eight or nine dollars a gallon. And ironically, sugar wasn't much lower then than it is now. It was ten or twelve dollars a hundred pounds then.

Well I dwindled around there, did some moonshining, worked with some other people awhile, and along in the mid-twenties worked in the oil fields awhile. Like I told you, two or three weeks before Christmas I'd come home, put up two or three little batches, and run it off. I knew a lot of customers round about, and always attempted to make it a little better than some of the competitors. I'd put it in charred oak kegs and let it age a little.

Finally, in 1929, I moved down on Caddo in the Big Lake camp area and built the house that's still standing. I lived there fifteen years, and about ten or twelve of those years, until liquor was declared legal again, I might near pretty well occupied a lot of my time out in the lake with my still mounted on a platform.

The method of operation was a comparatively small outfit. Over in Mississippi they would dig a hole in the side of a hill and put a still there that would hold several thousand gallons and make it in a big way and haul it off with trucks. But here, our method was mostly to put a platform out over the water in Caddo Lake in thickets where only a small canoe-like boat could get into, and run five or six barrels of mash.

You put water and hops and yeast cake together and then cook it in a container. Most everybody used oil drums by then, after cleaning 'em out good. There was 110-gallon drums could be had from an oil company in Shreveport. I had several of them, and some of them rusted out during the ten or fifteen years of operation. I maintained an outfit on a platform that I could set up on some sort of carpenter-type workhorses and then lay the decking down without making any noise establishing a location, like hammering and building a platform.

We usually used wood to burn, and put this drum into a brick furnace and fixed it up with this old chimney mud that you can get around here. It's a white-looking post oak clay. They mix grass with it and build mud chimneys. Anyway, we bricked it up, made a furnace, put a smokestack around the end of the drum, and it became a pretty efficient burner. Usually the best whiskey to be made is to boil it once and run your fluid out through a copper tubing in the lake—let the lake cool it—and back on the platform. After you'd run up a bunch of it, you'd put all that you've got back in your drum and run it again to get it real strong. You could get up to 170–180 proof, almost pure alcohol. Then you'd cut it down with, preferably, rainwater to where it's about 100 proof. After that you'd put it in charred oak kegs that you could buy anywhere and age it awhile. It was pretty good material. In fact, I expect it was as safe to drink as any they've got now.

Then it got to be that the price of the product was so low that we got to making it with a "thumper." A thumper is a smaller tank that sits between your copper boiler and the coil that goes in the lake to cool it. It acts sort of as a settling bulb. That way, at one run you can make pretty strong liquor. It's not as good as the complete double run, but it's pretty fair if you fire it slow.

Alcohol leaves fluid at 180 degrees. You seen the old-time car gauge where the heat indicator was painted red at 180 degrees? Well, at 180 degrees the old-time antifreeze would boil out of your radiator. Water don't make steam till it reaches 212 degrees; therefore, the secret of making good liquor was to keep your temperature between 180 and 212. Then only alcohol would come out and you wouldn't get boil-over of mash or non-alcohol. Some of 'em didn't know that, but I had a doctor friend who like the material I was making, and he showed me how to put a temperature gauge on it and to hold it in the proper perspective, or what they call now the proper quality control. Lots of people have told me that my product was as good or better than most.

The first couple of years at the lake I didn't incorporate my moonshining up again. I had a feeling I'd like to ignore it. But the Depression was on, and other people who hardly ever cared for a drink before was about ready to drink some. I tried to make it with just fishing and hunting and renting boats and cabins, but people kept on wanting to know why I didn't have whiskey. All the rest of the camps had it and was making big money out of it. In the end, so many of my doctor, lawyer, and preacher friends and all prevailed upon me that I fired up a sort of semiprivate affair, and for about seven or eight years there that was almost the mainstay, though I still fished and built duck blinds and duck-hunted and sold ducks. I guess those years and others like 'em made me a pretty good car driver. I never had a car wreck, and I think I became so alert during those days that I would see both ways nearly all the time. I got to where I would constantly look and watch, got in the habit of watching and seeing people and things. I managed through the years without getting completely captured, though I had a few brushes that didn't amount to much.

I could see pretty good, and I knew they couldn't out-paddle me in a bateau boat. I'd fire my engine up every morning before daylight. I burnt wood in it, mostly, and I'd build a fire before daylight and get it good and hot, and then go home and milk my cows and all. And part of the time I had it down the bank, where I could put on hip boots and walk through a corn patch I had planted right behind the barn and get on down the lake and squirrel hunt a little and wade out and check it and throw some more wood in it, and walk back.

For a good while there I called it a sideline, the liquor making, 'cause I built boats and fished and duck-hunted and sold ducks and fish, and also would work an oil field job that came close enough by. Then I had a garden and farmed some, kept a couple of milk cows and a wild hog in the woods, and I had a good squirrel dog. I stayed pretty busy and guess I enjoyed those fifteen years about as good as any.

I had a stationary platform out in the lake back in the thick cy-press timber, where only a small boat could get back in there. I main-tained that platform for years, and later got me another down the shoreline where it was wooded. There was quite a bunch of timber for three or four hundred yards back in there. I had me a platform made out of two workhorses—heavy scaffolding, a carpenter-line thing. Then I'd cover that with some boards, just laying 'em on it.

And it was movable. Sometimes, due to the water dropping in summer, it'd get too low to operate and I'd have to move back out to the island again. I could move it in my little paddle boat. I'd put one set of legs over on one side and the other set over the other. I moved one day when I was running stuff and got to Bear Island while it was still running. I carried over the barrels and two sets of horses, got the rig over there and set the barrels back up. When the still got through running, I dumped some of the hot stuff out into the boat and hauled it over to Bear Island and dipped it back into the barrel. Then, when it filled up again, I moved the next two horses to the rear of the plat-form and the still over there in time to fill it.

I had a kind of a canopy built over the top of the platform—the trees kind of pulled together. It was out in a cypress brake with pretty high trees. I was afraid an airplane would see it, though I guess in those days there wasn't nobody bothering you too much anyway. Later, I got to where I'd move these first horses over there in the summertime when the trees put out and would use that other set for the winter.

On the platform I had some brick laid there with a piece of old tank iron on it and a 110-gallon drum. I'd set it up and brick it and have a smokestack out of eight-inch pipe that had come from an old gin house. I'd fire it right under there on the side of the drum, and had a funnel here in the bunghole, a funnel that held five gallons, and a valve there, and let it stay on all the time. I'd put gunnysacks over it. And here on the other part of the platform I had a circle of six mash barrels.

I'd haul wood there and just leave it in my bateau and stick it right under the cooker from the boat. Then the discharge went to a little drum which set there, went into the bottom of it and come out the top. Then it went into the lake and curled around there and come up on the platform to the thumper. This means that this that you're boiling, as it goes through there, could drop below boiling, and your water would settle in this and your alcohol would keep going. You'd draw that off now and then and you'd get strong liquor, which went over into some kegs I had. From the thumper I had a piece of copper tubing run over there with a valve on it so I could heat this liquor. I'd put chips in it, them there burnt chips you bought from Arkansas. Then I'd get everything warm and move that tub and cover it with gunnysacks and tarpaulins to maintain the heat. It'd be thirty hours before the heat would be gone, and by then the whiskey would be done turned red and was ready for bottling. I'd take my jugs to the bateau and siphon it right out of this tub into my jugs and then go stash it close enough to the house to get rid of it. And by then I'd be making another run. I was a freewheeler!

Now, one other time I had some big-mouthed pickle jars, and I would put a batch of these oak chips from Arkansas, oak chips that had been charred a golden brown, in these pickle jars. I'd fill 'em with whiskey and set 'em on a little platform up above the big one that I'd made on the side of a tree. The sun would shine on it and heat it, and you could look at it and tell when it was ready. Then you'd just stick a hose over in there and draw it off into your jugs.

And I have aged whiskey in a box with just an ordinary house kerosene lamp that's burnt all the time. You'd have a ten-gallon and a five-gallon keg in this tight box, but you'd have to give it a little air in order to furnish oxygen to the lamp. It would heat that whiskey after a few days to where it was 80 or 90 degrees in there.

I've read where distillers would put whiskey on a boat and ship it overseas and back. The motion of the boat, rocking of the waves, splashes the whiskey in the keg and seems to enhance its flavor. One time, when the Galbraiths was carrying the U.S. Mail on the Caddo Lake mail boat, we put a five-gallon keg under the bow of his boat and let him make a few trips to see what happened. But I don't know if we could tell it made any difference in it. Finally, I quit using kegs and started using those charred chips.

Like I told you, I'd put some charcoal chips in a half a barrel and run the liquor right in on them, and run a little copper tubing from the thumper over to the aging machine and warm it. In two or three days it'd turn red and taste pretty good, good enough it wasn't no trouble to sell it. The main trouble was, it got down to two dollars a gallon, and was costing about fifty cents a gallon for the ingredients. Course, we didn't count our work anything then. I guess we called it pleasure.

I was always trying to improve the operation. I remember one time I was experimenting with an energy-saving rig. I had welded two drums together to make a kind of long affair, and had established a platform not too far down below the house, up in shallow water in a thicket where a boat wouldn't ordinarily go. I builded a furnace around it and had five barrels around it on this platform, and I soon proved that my experiment didn't work so good. It would smoke and was noisy. I had a firebox and kind of a "throat" on back under the last part of the drum, sort of like sawmill and gin boilers I had seen, and had it bricked up. But it was so close to the house that, on a cold, frosty morning, you could hear the thumper start bumping all the way to the house! But I had an irrigation pump set up there, a pipe-line run up to quite a large garden I had, and I'd rig up and fire that pump up and stick the exhaust pipe straight up so that you couldn't hear the thumper down there for the exhaust pipe on the irrigation engine. Course, I wasn't pumping water particularly, just trying to make noise!

The smell never did go anywhere other than right close by. I could smell pretty good because I never did smoke—haven't yet—and I never did notice a smell to amount to anything. Though sometimes, I guess, in those days I smelled like whiskey and duck and money and fish, all at the same time. I made quite a lot of drinking material. In fact, I kept a count one year, started at the first of the year and kept a count on the calendar, and by the middle of March I had made 385 gallons. That don't sound like much, but it's a pretty good deal of whiskey.

If you operated right, you could sell to doctors, lawyers, bankers, preachers, and people who really didn't want other people to know they were getting it. Or, you could make a pest out of yourself by not using it carefully and making poor stuff and getting in the wrong kind of company with it. But the sheriff liked good whiskey, you know! However, I don't know anybody in this county who actually had a deal with any of the law enforcement officers in order to get by. It might have been they was nice to them or took them a mess of fish or something, but as far as any actual payoff, I don't believe there ever was. The federal revenuers was the only ones the people in this area was actually afraid of. But this is a large area of Caddo Lake, with lots of swamps, shallow. water, and thick cypress trees where you could go back and build you a platform whereby an airplane couldn't even see it.

So, about getting caught, there was the game warden on one side and the revenuers and sheriff on the other, but I never did operate with anybody else and I guess most people didn't think I was doing it as much as I was. I mostly sold to doctors, lawyers, preachers, and people like that, and I never kept any around the house or had any drinking taking on. To come to my house you wouldn't think there was anything like that right down the lake. There weren't no drunks laying around there, no outward signs that I was doing much liquor business. My wife and children went to church, and I went some. I was pretty respectable; once I traded 100 gallons of moonshine for a car! I had some revenuers nip at me a few times, and the grand jury almost voted a bill against me once, but I carried the sheriff a mess of fish and I carried the game warden some whiskey. I didn't think it was ethical to carry the sheriff whiskey and the game warden fish! So I managed to squirm on by until it dwindled off and got over with, and I don't have any records in the courthouse to prove that what I'm telling you happened, but it did.

There were some people would get their stills tore up, though I never had one tore up. They would get brazen and put them out in open spots and let them get found, and of course they had to tear 'em up. They couldn't refuse to tear 'em up. To satisfy the Christian Temperance Union and the bootleggers too, they had to have a showing for both sides. It still goes on that way everywhere now; you scratch my back and I'll scratch yours, though I never did scratch many backs.

Most of the people, they would try to be big shots and would hire them some colored folks to help them do the work and wind up with a poorly built operation and steal from each other and get in trouble and get caught. One would tell on the other one just to act ugly. I didn't never piddle with anybody. In fact, theoretically, I wasn't even making whiskey. It just wasn't my line of business. I just built boats and farmed and had a garden and had hogs and had boats for rent, and all. But I had my still rigged up with six barrels.

My wife went to church all the time and carried the children, and my liquor making was a complete foreign thing away from other things. I entertained the preachers or the crooks, either one.

But the worst thing I ever got into, there was a roughneck over on the north side of the lake named Gent Griffis. His dad had killed a game warden, and his brother had killed a man named Williams in Mooringsport, for nothing, and got out of it. Gent was a pipeliner and claimed he was rough and tough, and he was. He showed up one Sunday with a friend of mine, old Hervey Gray, and a woman that I knew. I had just walked down to the lake and taken a drink of my choice liquor that I had stashed down at the edge of the water and dressed me a catfish. I was fixing to cook it for dinner. I didn't look for my wife to come back, since it was on Sunday. But Gent Griffis, Hervey Gray, and this woman showed up, and they had been prowling all night and was kind of groggy, but needed another drink bad to sober up on. We walked down to the platform and I gave 'em a drink. Then this Gent Griffis got to telling me how bad he was. I knew him but hadn't been seeing much of him. I tried to ignore him, but he kept getting annoysome, picking at me and threatening me, this, that, and another. Finally I told him, "Looks to me like I may have to straighten you out." Well, that just suited him, he wanted to be rough. So we walked out on the bank and lit into fighting. And while we was fighting, my wife and the preacher showed up, and was watching us!

Well, old Gent was short and tough and bull-necked, and wasn't as high as I was and had short arms. I had just had a couple of drinks to make me feel pretty good, and I could reach further than he could. Anyway, I was just out-beating the hell out of him, hitting him in the nose, face, and ears, and he wasn't doing no good about hitting me. If he could have hit me, he'd have hurt me. And this old boy, Hervey Gray, was kind of on my side. He says to Gent, "Now you picked the fight, it's up to you!" Finally, I busted his ear and it went to bleeding, and then I busted his nose. When he smelt that fresh blood it made him mad, and directly he charged into me and tore my shirt off, and I slammed him in the back a couple of good licks and he caved in over there on his knees. He got up about halfway crying and threatening to get his knife out, but Hervey Gray says, "Now you just behave, you just done got whupped and you just might as well behave yourself!"

Well, he mumbled around about how he might be back and I says, "Come back sometime and we'll fight two out of three and see who's the best!" They left, and he come back later and we was as good of friends as we'd ever been, which never was much. But he'd have whupped me if he could've reached me—he'd been drinking the night before and was too groggy and I could just outbox him. But the preacher seen how us poor folks lived.

Back yonder during Prohibition there wasn't a lot of trying to find stills. Mostly the stills that was destroyed was reported by some hunter or by somebody who was mad at you. And if you did found it tore up, you'd just put up another one. The main thing you'd try to save was the copper coil. You kept it and took off and the rest of the stuff was expendable. You could get you another drum and barrel and be back in business pretty quick if you had your copper coil—thirty or forty feet of half-inch pipe that you could run into a water barrel or down into the lake.

Finally, the revenuers began to come around and attempt to buy stuff. One time a man in Waskom who had formerly been a moonshine-buyer, and who had got captured, began to help 'em a little, we think. One day he joined a man from Tyler named McInturf, the revenuer, and they made a sweep through the Karnack area buying liquor all the way down to my place. They didn't come to my house, but stopped up above there, and this Waskom man come on down and wanted a gallon and a quart. That looked kinda funny, since he'd been buying it on credit or else I'd give it to him. Anyway, he give me the money. There was a man in town here, a very nice gentleman down there who wanted some ducks and some drinking material, and while I was getting his material this fellow went on back to await me coming with the gallon and a quart. I got his material and ducks and carried this gallon and a quart across a field there up to where the road turned around and put it under a bridge. I don't know, I didn't have any particular suspicion, but I happened to do that. So, before I had went on up to where they were, this fellow came back and wanted to know what happened. I told him and he went on, and apparently they picked it up.

Well, in about a week I had gone over in the oil field peddling fish and stayed all night over there with my brother, and when I got back to Marshall the next morning the streets was infested with moon-shiners, some of 'em out on bond, some of 'em not quite out. One fellow come up to me and says, "Wyatt, did you sell so-and-so any liquor day before yesterday?" I told him, "Naw," but it was the epi-sode where I put it under the bridge. I never did get to see the reve-nuer, or he didn't get to see me; anyway they didn't arrest me. I guess the evidence was a little too scattered about, and I had a witness I figured I could use.

In the end they got to chasing them with airplanes. Old Scottie Rainey was the liquor control agent, and he was pretty diligent. He got to flying with a National Guard fellow from Austin, and I told him—I'd quit making whiskey by then—"You oughtn't do people that way. You ought to chase a moonshiner in the same way of loco-motion. If he's in a car, you use a car. If he's walking, walk. If he's riding a mule, ride. It ain't fair to chase him in an airplane, because he hasn't got one." Well, they was flying and looking for stills one day and this plane crashed down there in the State Park. It killed the pi-lot and like to have killed Scotty. He told me when he saw me next, he says, "You were the first one I thought of when I hit the ground!"

There was bootleggers around, too. They'd get it for about a dollar a quart and sell it for two dollars a quart. It was customary for a boot-legger to sell to a customer and then have a drink with him to prove to him that he wasn't afraid of it either.

My uncle [Perry Bonner] was caught as a bootlegger. He was an un-educated person, except he could count money. He got into the moonshining and had a little store out in Karnack, but mostly he'd get other people to make it. Finally, he and his wife decided that if they'd move to Marshall they'd get richer faster, and it wasn't long before they had him in the penitentiary.

If he'd stayed on the lake where things was wild like he was, he would never have got caught. Once I went down there to try to spring my uncle and old man Artie Jackson from here, who had also got caught, but we didn't have no luck. Mr. Jackson had charge of the chicken house down at the Imperial Penitentiary Farm out of Houston on the Brazos. He says—Dan Moody was governor then—"Dan's all right. He never has refused me nothing, except, of course, I ain't asked him for anything yet."

A lot of my neighbors went to the Federal Correctional Institutes of Texarkana and Tyler, but somehow I managed to squirm by. I guess you might say I'm really the only uncaught one in the area. I don't attribute it to anything uncanny, except that maybe there didn't as many people know about me as I thought. People wanted to know, "Wasn't I scared?" And I told 'em, "Yessir, I'm scared, I stay scared." Maybe that's the reason I didn't have any trouble. I had a grand jury vote to bill me once, but I got underground wind of it and pulled a few strings that night, and the next day they voted that they didn't have enough evidence for conviction and believed they'd throw it out. I never did have a trial.

VIII

During those years at the lake a lot of other things went on besides moonshining. I kept cows and milked cows almost twice a day for years. We had a Delco Electric Plant, and I'd work in the oil fields and around, and one day I got me a piece of an old machine wheel, the part that you pump with your feet that turns the head of the machine. I rigged it up on a board, and made me some belts around about, and had it reduced down in the gear ratio, and built a stroke, and built kind of a walking beam affair like on a pumping well, and rigged my churn under the end of this walking beam. And that thing would churn away! You could hook the churn up and pull the switch and it'd start in a hurry—had a thirty-two-volt motor on it off the Delco battery light plant. It'd squeal and take on and slide some before it would finally get to churning. When you'd turn it on, the motor on that Delco would kick on with that first load, and after it got to rolling good the Delco would stop and the batteries would keep it going. Poeple would come for miles around to see that 'lectric churn go.

And once I had hogs that had little ones out in the pen on a hot day, and I rigged a spray up so I could spray water on the edge of the barn and help cool 'em off. I also determined I could set up an electric fan out there that run on the Delco and fan air over the hogpen. A fellow come along and looked at that and shook his head, says, "I've heard of this air conditioning, but this is the first time I've ever seen an air-conditioned hawg pen."

Besides the hogs I had around the house, I always run hogs in the woods. At one time in this country, the Big Thicket and lots of East Texas and Louisiana was free range. We let cows and hogs run in the woods here until around 1930. Later, it was a sort of local option affair, where some sections had voted to keep the animals up, and some were still using the old free range system.

People over in Marion County, the Walkers and the Carters among 'em, who owned land out on the edge of the hills, would turn a few hogs in the woods, an old sow and a boar hog or two. They had a claim in the woods. The hogs would mix up with each other, and along in the spring, like the old free range cattle days in the West, the Walkers and the Carters would build a pen with a trapdoor and bait the hogs into it and catch them. And the ones that were following hogs with their mark on they would mark and castrate. Then in the winter they would catch them down in the woods for butchering.

The environment was such that these hogs would get long and lean and sinewy and wasn't too much of a meat hog, called "pine rooters." Those old pine rooters would root around a little pine tree and root it up and eat the root of it. They would graze around the edge of the lake and pick up mussels, and eat worms and acorns and the roots of briars and some green stuff. In the wintertime they'd get fat when you got a good acorn crop. A fat acorn-fed hog would taste pretty good, but when you fried him, lots of him would go greasy and not remain solid like a corn-fed hog. These pine rooters would get big tushes—they wasn't high-bred hogs—and among the hog family they was like the longhorn was among Texas cattle. Pine rooters were acclimated to the environment and the climate. You couldn't hardly catch one. They would herd together, and when a dog went there they'd kill him if he didn't watch. I had a dog that would catch a hog. He'd grab him by the ear and then lean against him and bite his ear, and the hog would squeal. You could gather him by the hind legs then, and tie him down.

Mostly they'd catch 'em in the winter. I've been over in there when there would be hogpens scattered all through the woods. They'd come to the pen in a wagon, catch the hogs, and carry 'em home. Then, out on the edge of the hills, they'd quarantine 'em a little while before they killed 'em. Sometimes, maybe, they'd kill a wild one in the woods. I have killed a loose hog or two across the river along in the late twenties. We were making whiskey up the river one day, and I went over and killed a nice shoat, and another fellow killed a squirrel or two, and Edward Hartzo fished a net, and we had a big picnic down there, with plenty of good fresh drinks right out of the still before we eat.

I was trapping hogs as late as fifteen years ago. Over in the Harrison Bayou area there were hogs that had drifted off from farmers and had went wild inside the government reservation of Harrison Bayou. I mentioned to one of the fellows that owned one, "Let's go over there and try to catch it." "Well," he said, "I've got other hogs and it ain't worth the trouble to try." I said, "Well do you mind if I get one?" "No," he said, and gave up on it.

So I shot one down there and brought it home, but he was thin and ill-fed. But there was an old sow that had pigs that I had discovered, and there was a younger sow or two. All told, there was thirty-some-odd hogs up past the bayou. I enlisted the help of a younger person here, Bill Wadlington, and we went up the bayou in the government reservation and built a log pen out of local-cut timber about three feet high. On one end we cut a hole and established a sliding door that you could pick up, and put a beam over a stake in the pen, and back behind cut a notch in it, and tied it down to a stake—hooked it into a stake—and tied an ear of corn on it. Then we scattered shelled corn out of the pen and out around in the woods. Well, we caught hogs nearly every time we went there until we finally caught over thirty. The little ones that were in there, we'd put in the bottom of the boat in an enclosure there that's sort of a water box, and we'd nail a board over it until we got to the house where we had the trailer down at the Big Lake Camp. The old sow and the bigger hogs, we'd tie both feet together and stick a pole through them and carry 'em to the boat and lay 'em in the boat with this pole still through 'em. We brought home thirty-some-odd.

Well, we ate some and sold some in Longview. We left an old sow and a medium-size male for future purposes. At that time my brother-in-law [Travis Hayner] was running Big Lake Camp, which is where we would operate from, and he told me later, "Somebody, so-and-so, killed your other two hogs up there, so you ain't got no seed left in the woods." And that's the last that were up there.

Another thing I did a lot of back in my years at the lake was duck hunting. In the teens, before the dam was built, it was customary for a duck hunter to have him a pump gun. That way he could shoot lots. He would go out around the lake where it had been dry in the summer and water had come up over the grass and all, and there were seed there, and he would back up under a tree and just stick a stool in the ground. He had a round stool like a Japanese milk stool, and he'd just stick it in the ground and set there. There'd be enough of ducks fly in and fly by where he could get all the shooting he needed.

Then, as time went on and a few more lakes began to be built in the area—Caddo at one time was the only lake in this country—the ducks became a little scarcer and they got to building duck blinds and putting out live decoy ducks. Out in town, lots of people raised decoys. And they imported "English callers," it was advertised, to mix with the "clabberheads" and make smaller and better-calling decoy ducks. Unless you had about fifteen, you didn't consider you was in business much, and some people would keep up to forty or fifty. The more live ducks you put out, the more so it'd attract the wild ducks. I've killed sixty-four ducks in one day, shooting over decoys.

The Galbraith brothers both was big duck hunters, and their favorite blind was a cypress tank you'd buy back yonder. The tank was about three-and-a-half feet at the bottom and tapered up pretty good, built out of cypress staves. They'd go out there and put it just above the waterline. They'd drive stakes down and put two of the tanks side by side. They'd put a hunter in one and a hunter in the other, with a little cypress brush straight up around 'em. They were dinky little things, but they'd last; they were built out of cypress. They were made by the Cypress Tank Company to go on a water well, or something.

So that was their method of hunting, and they learned way back in the early days that if you put enough decoys out, all the ducks would come to that big bunch. You put two, three hundred decoys out, person up yonder with thirty or forty decoys won't have no ducks go over him. They'll all go to that big bunch.

And they built motorboats almost especially for duck hunting, like Galbraith's *The African Queen*, with a cab over the front where you could walk up under and set down. When you was out in the lake you'd throw a line over a stump, and it would face the wind, and would be fairly warm in there. They'd get out there, and Mr. Dixon and Fred Wappler and Andy Carson would shoot ducks with them nine-shooting pumps and automatics, and kill 'em by hundreds.

They would hear of a norther coming over the Western Union in Marshall, and there would be an exodus of T-Models to the lake that night in the cold weather and through the mud holes. We'd hear 'em passing all night, and Papa would say, "Well, we'd better kill a hog in the morning, there's a norther coming." When I moved to the lake in '29, I kept ducks for decoys and we'd rent blinds with ducks for the hunters to use. They had a limit of twenty-five then, which was way too high. I had brothers who was younger than me, and some of them got married at the time and lived with us on the lake. Usually somebody was there, so we maintained somebody in the duck blind all the time. People would come and buy ducks, and if I got a surplus I'd haul 'em down below Shreveport to a gambling roadhouse affair, those days what you might call a "speakeasy" up in the East. They had roulette wheels, poker tables, and carrying on's at some old plantation house below Shreveport. Fellow by the name of Cockerham said he'd take all the ducks I could carry. I'd get six bits apiece for mallards and pintails, fifty cents apiece for black ducks and smaller ducks. We didn't kill many teal. We'd kill a good many what you call "blackjacks," but most of 'em was mallards or pintails, which is a big duck, or redheads.

Old man Taylor wasn't much into the duck business. Sometimes he'd have an order for a duck or two, maybe four or five, or he'd buy a duck or two and either sell it or give it to somebody. It wasn't unusual for you to bring people ducks. You didn't have much refrigeration them times but the weather, and you had to keep 'em moving, but a duck will keep four or five days pretty good if the weather is cool. I had a little store down on the lake, a twenty-six-foot-long building about twelve feet wide, built out of one-by-twelve planks, and I have had a duck hanging on every plank around it at one time. It was snowing and I was wondering what I was going to do with them, and killing more. We'd eat gizzards and livers out of ducks down there one winter, four or five of us, until we was burnt out on it. We'd sell the ducks and eat the livers and gizzards, which is a delicacy.

There was a fellow up here in Tennessee named Nash Buckingham who wrote articles about what they called "jump shooting." Well, we called that "bushwhacking" at Caddo Lake. He wrote in an article in the *American Rifleman* that he put a loop of string around his paddle and put it over his shoulder, so that if a duck jumped up he just turned the paddle loose and grabbed his gun. Well, I had a different version of it. Papa used to put a loop over his paddle and just turn the paddle loose when a duck jumped and let it be hanging there, one side or the other, but I never did like that. For years in my bateau paddle boat, which I've killed a lot of ducks from—and the way I like to hunt you can kill squirrels, ducks, deer, anything out of the boat—I would carry two paddles. Keep one laying in the boat and use one, and when them ducks fly up just forget everything and get your gun. When you get through shooting, you got you a paddle to go back and pick the other paddle up and chase the cripples if you got any. So I wrote this to the National Rifle Association and referred to Mr. Buckingham's article and they run it in there.

I never killed many geese on Caddo. The main goose hunting took place back in the days before the dam. Geese would roost out on the Big Lake and would come and feed at night in the moonlight. People would hide on the small feeding grounds and be there when the moon came up and the geese would start coming. I was too young for those days, but heard the old-timers talk about it.

I've killed some geese, I've killed some old honkers, and when I lived at the lake I'd kill a goose every once in a while—a brant, not an old honker, but a brant. When them geese are going over the lake, they'll be a goose leave 'em now and then and go to the water. There's two kinds that leave the herd and go to the water. One of 'em's too poor to fly and the other's too fat to fly. You won't see a medium-meated goose leave the herd.

I'd watch for 'em at Long Point, or somebody else would see 'em, and we'd see one drop out now and then. Then I'd get somebody to run the boat and I'd get right up in the bow and we'd take off right towards him wide open. He'd probably be in the lilies, but we would run a boat road nearly till we got to him if we could, and I could warn the colored man running the boat, "Now, don't stop to knock them lilies off, 'cause we won't get nothing. Long as it'll go, keep going!" And every once and a while I'd kill a goose there, early in the fall. And he'd be real fat, usually, a speckled goose. I'd leave him out there for a while and pick him up in a bateau.

Have I told you how the Galbraiths killed 'em in the daytime down on Big Lake? The Galbraiths was very efficient in rigging up ways to catch and kill. There was two or three big hollow stumps out in the big old water in Louisiana on the other side of Big Green Brake, where the geese would raft, as you call it—just sit out there in the daytime and wait until night to feed. In the fall of the year, when the geese come in, there wasn't hardly no closed season then, they'd light down there in that big open water. A goose ain't going to light close to nothing that a boat can hide behind. A goose ain't crazy as a duck. He looks like he's crazy and he acts crazier, but he's got some smartness about him. Well, they would go down there before daylight, and one of the Galbraiths would get in that hollow stump with a nine-shooting automatic shotgun, that Remington Model 11, and the other one would just get in a bateau and go over to the other side of the lake and start fishing. The day before they'd stretched four trotlines away from this stump in four different directions—way out there, two or three hundred yards to a quarter of a mile. The strings would have corks on 'em, wooden corks about every eight or ten feet apart, just enough to keep the thing afloat. These were wooden corks, what you call "perchneck" corks, about three inches big around and just plain wood. They'd order them from the Linden Thread Company.

So a string with corks on it would be stretched way out four ways from the stump. One of the Galbraiths would put the other one in the stump, then he'd go out in the bateau boat and get beyond the geese and piddle around and fish and just gradually ooze towards these geese. He'd be out there a quarter of a mile from 'em. They weren't particularly scared of him. He'd just doodle around, fish over here and fish over there, just enough to make 'em move. So they'd swim away from him without flying, and they'd go one way and they'd come to this trotline with the corks on it. They wouldn't cross it, so they'd swim back the other way until they come to this other string. He'd gradually oodle them geese up in one fork of this trotline. And as they got nearer the stump, the two lines were closer together, and finally they'd swim up to that stump close enough for Galbraith to massacre 'em! That was their method of laying it on 'em.

I still love to hunt, and them old green-head mallards is the ones I like to frustrate. They're sharp, I mean to tell you! Down on the south shore one year, between Jones and Swanson's Landing, I would ooze up that shore the very particularist I could wading with hip boots on, and after while I'd see one's head way up yonder, sticking up. I'd be stopped and he'd be stopped and I'd try to stand there till he moved. But he knew, he'd done seen me! Finally one day, I didn't wade up the shore, but got out on the bank about where I'd been seeing 'em. I oozed out there down on my knees, oozed along in the edge of the water on my knees, and oozed out there and got up on two of 'em. I killed one, but you know, that other rascal wouldn't fly! He went around in them trees and he'd jump and swim but wouldn't fly. I didn't get him, but if he'd have flew I'd have killed him. He knew better than to get up in the air. He wasn't crippled, either.

IX

I guess what I done and what I been accused of covers everything, you put 'em both together. But there's almost always a loophole around any law, or a way around most any occasion that you get into. In fact, I think sometimes of the tights I been in and the alibis that I have had to come forth with, and I always do better when I'm completely surprised and don't have an answer at all and need to tell a big lie. It comes to me better than if I have time to plan it ahead. It won't work planned ahead—the question won't fit the lie—so you end up having to save your lies till the question arises.

Well, that brings up my closest brush with the law. Fishing was pretty good at my camp in the thirties. Lots of people would come get fish, get drinking material, and to fish some themselves. But in the spring of the year we'd have a closed season, whereby you couldn't fish for white perch March and April. That applied for several years, but Louisiana wasn't closed, and we recognized it to some extent. The fishermen couldn't fish in those months, but 'long about March of 1931 the game warden was bringing some Louisiana licenses down to my camp and leaving them for some of the courthouse bunch from Marshall to come down and get their license and go to Louisiana and fish, which gave 'em a limit of twenty-five fish a day on each license caught in Louisiana. It was recognized as being an up-and-up procedure, which it was. The game warden was just helping the sheriff's department in Louisiana sell licenses for the convenience of the people here. Mr. Roscoe Russick was game warden, and he had a helper, Mr. Frank Vannest, a local man. Mr. Vannest was my friend, all right, and I was glad he was on the game warden force because he'd come down to the house without the other game warden and I'd find out things.

Well, those licenses were only good for a week, and didn't cost much, but I didn't buy any because I didn't see that I needed 'em. But this particular morning on Friday the thirteenth of March—you'll look at the calendar some day you'll find that in 1931 Friday came on the 13th of March—I got up real early and went out on the lake and doubled up a hoop net with a wing on it I had out, and caught a bunch of fish. Then I went by a box and poured out a few more in the boat—didn't count 'em, but they were all big ones. Anyway I made a lot of noise out there, 'bout getting daylight. I had a lantern light with me and some scales, and I weighed the fish up and strung 'em in two- and three-pound packages. That was so I wouldn't have to weigh 'em when I was selling 'em. I could pick out two, four, three, five, seven, any amount on up, and I could sell 'em right quick. I'd learnt that by a fellow in town that got convicted of selling fish on the strength that he had weighing scales in his car.

Anyway, this particular morning it was a little late, and my plans was to carry the fish to Louisiana. Ordinarily I'd come to the bank and load 'em in a sack down the bank and then get ready and drive down there and grab 'em and go to Shreveport with 'em. I'd ordinarily drive up the road and check the game warden, then run back and grab my fish and go, but this morning I got kind of brave and threw all these fish up in a wheelbarrow out on the pier. And just as I rolled 'em to the bank, two game wardens stepped down from the edge of the lake. They'd been up there behind the next house. They said, "Look like we've trapped you," and I said, "Do, don't it." We talked a little and I began to look for loopholes, if there was any. Lawyers call 'em "technicalities," but us common criminals call 'em loopholes!

The game wardens started counting the fish, I don't know why, but after they counted 'em they started counting 'em again, and I watched 'em that time. There was forty-seven head, and I begin to see one loophole already. You was allowed two days' limits of game, them days, and I didn't quite have that. I thought on that a little, but I couldn't see where it'd help me any. I talked to 'em a little, and they said they was going out on the lake and find my net and check my fish box. I said, "All right." I didn't have any net out. I'd done doubled it up and throwed a big piece of something on it. I'd just stretch it out at night. I told 'em, "Well, could it be arranged where I might could just meet y'all in town? I need to milk my cow and shave before I go to jail." They agreed I could. As soon as they left and got out in the lake a ways, I went through the house, it was seven-thirty then, and put on some slightly different clothes. My wife and little baby still in the bed didn't know I was having a brush with the authorities. I thought on the matter a little, and I got in my old A-Model Ford coupe and took off for Shreveport.

Well, when the sheriff's office opened in the courthouse, I was standing in front of the window where they sold fishing licenses. I needed a shave bad, and I felt kind of bad too. I noted a name there on the window, a Mr. Pitchford. I had known a Pitchford some fifteen years before down in Louisiana in the oil fields, and I called the old man's attention to it. "Yes," he said, "that was one of my cousins." We got up a little conversation, and I told him, "Me and my wife is down here from Texas visiting friends in Shreveport and they want to go on a fishing trip somewhere out here." I says, "I understand you can get a week's license here?" "Yes," he said, "we have those licenses. We don't sell many of 'em." I says, "Well, we'd better get some, I guess. We don't want to get in any trouble down here in Louisiana."

So he got his book down and started getting ready to write, and I says, "What day of the month is this?" He kind of chuckles and says, "This is Friday the thirteenth." I says, "I don't want to be superstitious, but it's early this morning. Couldn't you date them yesterday? I've had some bad things happen to me on Friday the thirteenth." "Well," he says, "that'll butcher up my record." I says, "You said you didn't sell many, you didn't sell any yesterday, did you? Just let it go on yesterday." He seemed to weaken a little then, and I came forth with more excuses and mentioned the fact that I guess I better get one for my wife too, because she might be fishing some. He went over and talked to this other fellow a little, and they kind of laughed. He come back over and said that they guess it'd be all right to date 'em the day before. So he began to write 'em, and I got so nervous I couldn't hardly keep from ramming my hand under that little iron window and grabbing that first one he wrote out, but I managed to hold myself back. Soon as he got 'em wrote I thanked him profusely and already had the money shoved way under there for 'em. They was about $1.50 apiece, something like that.

After I got those licenses I tore out to Waskom and got a shave and came on to Marshall. I went in the courthouse and encountered Mr. Ben Woodall, who was assistant county attorney. I knew Ben. He'd been down to the house some. He mentioned how come me in town so early? And I told him I run up to get a few things done and get back to work. I mentioned the fact that Russick the game warden brought licenses down there for Ross Faulkner and Frank Green, and they fished over in Louisiana. Yes, he said, he understood that, and it was all right and so forth.

Well, when the game wardens showed up I was setting there with my feet practically up on the county attorney's desk. They proceeded to want Ben to file charges against me, and that was when Mr. Ben Woodall discovered why I was there in the first place! He said, "Wyatt, I didn't know you were in trouble." I says, "I'm not. I've got two licenses and didn't have but forty-seven head of fish. Me and my wife both fished the day before with Frank Galbraith over in Louisiana." The game warden wanted to know why I didn't show 'em to 'em earlier? I said, "You didn't ask me about 'em." He got pretty hot, then, and said, "I'm gonna charge you with possession for purpose of sale." Well, that made me mad. I says, "Why don't you file charges against them other fellows for purpose of sale? They had fish just like me." He got real nervous and started to shaking and Ben Woodall says, "Y'all can't hardly fight it out here!" Anyway, in filing the charges, Ben Woodall didn't put down possession for purpose of sale, but just possession. They got the charge wrote out and bond made, and I went over to Mr. Frank Scott's, and he says, "Well, we'll just make bond."

The trial was held in Mr. John Henderson's court four days later. Mr. Sam Hall came over there to defend me, but he didn't offer any rebuttal evidence, and the justice of the peace stuck me a fine and cost. Hall says, "That's all right. You were going to be convicted anyway. We'll just appeal it in the county court."

Anyway, we made bond again, and the next thing was to appeal it to county court. I went on home. You had ten days to appear, and eleven days later Mr. Russick, the game warden, showed up and told me, "The lawyers didn't appeal your case. You'll have to go to jail or pay a fine." I says, "I left them under the impression that they'd appeal!"

We got to the courthouse in town about noontime, and while we was there I suggested I'd like to see my lawyer and started walking out. The game warden looked like he started to stop me, but says, "Hurry back." So I went and told Mr. Frank Scott what kind of shape they've got me in, and he got kind of alarmed. I says, "I'm going to jail. You done let me get in this shape." He says he'll get after me pretty quick.

While we were in the courthouse we found out that the chief of police, Easdale, had caught some of my neighbors from Karnack, Charlie Hale and John Post, and had 'em in jail for selling fish, and was hunting Edward Hartzo. Hartzo wasn't with 'em right at the time, but was still at large there in town trying to make bond for the other two before they put him in jail too.

So we went on down to the jail and clanged the door behind me, and it shore sounded loud! I told my friends, Charlie and John, "I just come down here to see y'all," hoping Scott would come and get me pretty quick. Well, the inmates of the jail, dopeheads and stuff, started to hollering, "Kangaroo court!" They'd already taken five dollars apiece off of Charlie and John. I kept trying to kill time and convince myself I could make it until Mr. Frank Scott transferred me, but I was pretty well shook up. Anyway I had companionship, birds of a feather! Finally, before the dopeheads got me, the jailer come back and announced that Scott had come to get me. Then those dopeheads saw that I'd escaped.

So we went back up to the courthouse, and there was the county judge, Mr. Lindsey, John Taylor the rough county attorney, Mr. Ben Woodall, two game wardens, Mr. Frank Scott, and about all the people you could think of. They was holding what they called a "mandamus hearing," arguing over whether to let my appeal go through or whether to call the case closed and make me pay or go to jail. Finally, John Taylor, this vicious prosecutor, wouldn't give in to deciding right then. He voiced the opinion that he'd need a day or two to study the law on it. Mr. Frank Scott says, "You mean you want to put my man back in jail here for three or four days while you decide a little issue like that?" Hartzo had got John and Charlie out by then, and they appeared on the scene. And when I heard 'em talking about jail again, I started oozing out and told 'em, "Fellows, I got a way to get home here, and when y'all get this settled just let me know and I'll be right on up here and do whatever you decide." The game warden looked at the other game warden and the others looked at the others and nobody actually said "Stop," so I squirmed away and come home.

The next day I went up there and went in Mr. Frank Scott's office and he was laughing. He says, "It's a good thing you left yesterday when you did. They was fixing to put you back in that jail!" I believed him, and them dopeheads probably would've killed me down there.

Anyway, they decided to let the case go to county court. That was in March, and they piddled along and set it for a month from then. But on the day they was supposed to try it, the game wardens got an anonymous call that there was a truck stuck over in Marion County with a load of fish on it, so they didn't come. We finally tried it in September. I was firing a boiler then out on the Haggerty place, a wildcat-drilling well out there they'd rigged up, but I got off and come to town for the trial. The prosecution had a weatherman there to prove it was too rough for me to have been on the lake the day before, like I claimed. But that just suited my lawyers fine, and they went to talking about, "Too rough for *him* to go on the lake? He'll go out there anytime!" They made a good issue out of that, and we produced a license to show I could legally fish, too.

So, after what evidence they could scrape up together on it, Mr. John Taylor the prosecutor made one of his eloquent speeches. He put his hand in his pocket and raised his leg way up high and shook his finger in my face; in fact, he made me feel real good. He put it on like a murder case, and I kinda fancied myself as an Al Capone, or something, the way he was laying things on. Then the jury went out, and we gave 'em the two licenses to look at, and they was back pretty quick. Justice had at last prevailed!

Mr. John Taylor was a pretty good prosecutor. He never lost many cases. He went on to Longview and stayed over there a few years, and several years later him and Little Joe Bibb was down at the lake one day before I sold my place in the late fifties. They had played out of liquor, and I invited them to go down to the house and look up in the ceiling of my old house and get some material that had been up there quite awhile.

While we were enjoying sipping that, Mr. John Taylor looked at me and says, "Wyatt, don't I recall having the pleasure of prosecuting you once?" "Well, yeah," I says, "I guess so, if you want to call it a pleasure. But if you recall a little closer you might remember having the displeasure of losing the case, too!"

X

Another episode that occurred during the thirties took place over at the Jap's camp. The Jap was quite a well-known figure. Lots of people came to see him. He had a lot of friends; I don't believe he had any enemies. He was a nice gentlemanly type of person. In those days, when I had just made a run and was waiting for the next mash to get ready on my platform out in the lake, I'd go over to the Jap's about once a week while the mash was working. I had an awful good squirrel dog, and the Jap liked squirrel and could cook 'em to perfection. He could cook anything, in fact, and kept all kinds of fine spices and things to put with 'em. I'd go over to the Jap's about eight or eight-thirty in the morning after I'd milked my cows and got the fishermen off, and I'd set a little of my best refreshments on the Jap's table. He'd be gone fishing for a while, and I'd go in the woods squirrel hunting. I'd kill three or four or five old fox squirrels and come back. Then through the middle of the day we'd have a few nips along and he'd fry 'em to perfection, and we'd have squirrel dinner.

Most of the time, there was someone would show up at the Jap's camp through the day and join us. In later years there was a friend of the Jap's named Jim Keeling, who spent time with him for the last few years of his life, and he'd be there. But another of the people who would visit the Jap was one Butch Jarrott from Shreveport, who was the state's official hangsman. He'd come over to the Jap's, and they'd come over to my house wanting refreshments, and maybe I'd go back over there with 'em. Over a period of two or three years Jarrott would come up intermittently. Apparently these hanging was kinda dwelling on him, because he'd carry a little piece of rope and constantly talk about hanging and show me how to tie the knot, and how you could put it on 'em where it'd break the neck, or put it on 'em so they'd just kick themselves to death, and choke. He'd drink and talk about that. During this time I had known of a case where a man and a woman had killed the woman's husband over at Hainesville. Jarrott told me the details of when he hanged those two people. Apparently they had been getting a few aspirin each day from the jailer and saved 'em up till the day of the hanging, then took 'em all. They was in such a stupor that they didn't really get to witness their own hanging very well. He told me about that. He got fifty dollars a head for hanging 'em. Butch Jarrott later died confined to his bed in New Orleans, but he already had the heebie-jeebies when I knew him.

Another visitor to the Jap was old man Moore, a blacksmith, who was constable at Mooringsport. He weighed 245 pounds and was all muscle. One day I encountered Mr. Moore at Mooringsport and had to look way up at him. He wasn't a mean person, but he liked to put on the impression that he was in a kind of smirking way, just to see what you'd say. And he was big enough to back up whatever he wanted to put on.

While I was talking to him this time, a little short, bow-legged colored man came running up to him wanting him to go over across a slough there and do something about some other coloreds. Mr. Moore slowly and nonchalantly told him, "You go back on over there and do so-and-so. My trigger finger's just been itching to kill me a damn nigger for several days, and I'll be over there after while." I know he probably never did go to see anything more about this man, but the fact that he give him authority to spread that news probably cleared up the whole matter.

But that was old man Moore. Along in the thirties, while I was visiting over at the Jap's a good deal, there was some boys from Mooringsport that had moonshine operations over in Big Green Brake, and one day I went over there. The fellow with me, Jimmy Hall, was the same man that was with me when my uncle drowned. We was camped out down there close to the Jap and went over to visit one day in early spring. When we got to the Jap's, there was the two would-be alleged moonshiners visiting there, and also this Mr. Moore the constable. Moore was there under the pretense of checking for moonshining. Well, these boys had gotten him in the house and got him pretty well liquored up. By the time we came, he was setting down on the pier, astraddle of the walk, so drunk he couldn't get up. We started visiting back and forth with Mr. Moore, and he had a .45 army automatic pistol and kept reaching down and catching ahold of it like he wanted to shoot somebody. Apparently he couldn't get up. I went down and talked to him a little, and in the struggle I managed to mention his gun and help him look at it and slipped the magazine out of it and worked the hull out of the barrel and give it back to him. I said, "Here, Mr. Moore, give 'em hell!" I was afraid he'd hurt somebody, maybe me!

Well, Jimmy Hall went down there and was popping off to him about something. Jimmy was a rather small person, and somehow or another we looked down there and Moore had Jimmy by his head, with his head pushed down on the walk, and was mashing his head. The back end of Jimmy was pointed toward the house and it was whirling around like a possum when you put an axe handle on his neck. I thought he was going to kill him before he got loose. And that old man tore all the hide off the back of Jimmy's neck. Blood was coming out from under the roots of the hair. Oh, he was stout, that big old blacksmith! Anyway, we went down there and got Jimmy aloose and he come back to the house and got mean after he got aloose from him, but he wasn't mean enough to go back down there. The Jap had a big fine wood inboard motorboat there, thirty feet long, with a big V-type windshield on it. About that time, the old man got up some way or 'nother and staggered around there and near about fell off one side and off the other, and finally fell headlong over into this glass windshield, and broke it. He cut his arms and face deep, blood just gushed out. Well, we immediately run down there and grabbed some sheets for bandages and got him in the boat, and the Jap fired it up and took off for Mooringsport about six miles away. When we got there, old man Jim Keeling, an old Spanish-American War veteran, was camped down there at the lake where the Jap landed. We got somebody to take him up to the doctor's office. Later Mrs. Moore heard about this ruckus and come down to the lake and asked Mr. Keeling in a very humble manner—she'd heard he got shot—she says, "Mr. Keeling, who shot my husband?" He says, "Mrs. Moore, John Barleycorn." She thought a moment, then says, "Mr. Keeling, who is he?" She didn't know who John Barleycorn was, but I guess most of you people know. But Mr. Moore got all right.

Speaking of constables, it may seem amazing to you, but back yonder around 1940 I was elected to the big office of constable of the Karnack and Uncertain precinct. I still lived over yonder at Big Lake Camp at that time, and was working in the oil field and building boats and making whiskey and building duck blinds and hunting and selling fish and ducks and stuff, all at once. I was constable and one of the most respected moonshiners of the area at the same time!

Once while I was constable, I got a call that there had been a fracas the night before down here at the colored school on the way down towards Leigh. There'd been a fight among the colored boys there. So, I got what dope I could on it before I left home, and there was this family of Charles lived around the lake. They called one of 'em "Buddy" and one of 'em "Pine Knot," and old man Jim Charles had several daughters and stuff. One of 'em got massacred down there; I think Beer Smith did that.

Anyway, I went down to the school and I first found the victims of the ruckus. Most of 'em had their heads skinned, their jaws broke and one boy had most of his teeth gone. This Buddy Charles down at the lake was the one had torn 'em up, and had cut a bunch of 'em. So I went down and told him I wanted the knife that he had used on them boys, and he handed it to me. It was a Boy Scout knife with a corkscrew in it, and a fork and knife and some other blades. And that thing had hair, blood, and guts still all mixed in it! He'd never even wiped it up. I put it in a napkin and kept it for evidence, but it wasn't long before old Bert Willmore who owned Shadey Glen Camp got him out of it. Pretty soon some other coloreds killed him in Marshall. He was a smart-alec and some bigger ones than him jumped on him and got rid of him.

Then there was the episode of Son Cutrer. I had a trouble call from up here at Uncertain. There were two or three beer-selling places across the river from Johnson's Ranch. Some of 'em were "floaters" and some of 'em were builded on permanent pilings driven in the ground. Mrs. Dovey McCord, who still resides right here on Taylor Island, lived at and operated one beer place over there. There was a man in Marshall named Son Cutrer, who I had worked in the T.P. [Texas & Pacific] shops with several years before, and he was mean and arrogant. Well, he had then went to work as a mechanic with some garage there in Marshall, and this particular morning, when he got off of the night shift, he and another fellow and a woman named Imogene had commandeered one of Ford Farr's taxicabs and started off on a party. They went to drinking and came on down several places and they run 'em off, and they finally wound up here at Uncertain. They went over to Dovey McCord's beer place and eat some breakfast with the taxicab waiting over on this side of the river, and they come back over there and engaged in a free-for-all fight and whupped the taxicab man until he left his cab. And then this Son Cutrer kicked the dash out of it, tore up the instrument board, and generally wrecked it! I learned later he had tore up the taxicab office in Marshall a week earlier than that, and beat holes in a brick wall with a table leg, and pretty well established himself as a rough character.

We, when I got over here, there was the taxicab setting up there wrecked, and down next to the river was a car left setting there with Son Cutrer in it asleep, and I presume drunk. I viewed him a little and then went across the river and they briefed me on the happenings. He'd already fractured the skulls of this woman and the man that had been with him, and they'd went off down the lake somewhere and caught a way back to town.

After I learned the particulars of the case, I went back over to the other side, and all the people around gathered to see me capture Son Cutrer. I looked him over, and he was laying there in the car, about ten-thirty in the morning on a hot day, and directly he roused up. People over at the beer joint across the river was watching him to see whatever measures I took to get him to town.

I told him, I says, "Son, I didn't know that was you laying there." I says, "I'm piddling around up here. I think all the people that was with you done went off and left you. I've got to run into town for a little while; if you want a ride to town you're welcome to go with me." Well, he rubbed his eyes a little and yawned and kind of looked blank and got in the car and away we went. And we were nearly to jail before he realized that he was incarcerated! If he had resisted arrest I was just going to agree with him and go ahead on and send him word to meet me in town, or something. I don't know what I'd have done.

Later, during the building of the war plant, long up in the spring of '42, Karnack got a mass of people in it. There was even a parking lot problem. People would get parked in behind and couldn't get out till the others come back. There was people living all through the woods here, in tents and all. We had a picture show, four or five eating houses, boarding houses, and some halfway bootleg joints. That's when I quit the constabulary. I decided it'd be better to join 'em than to oppose 'em.

XI

We moved from down at the lake about '43, but I still had the house about four or five years before I sold it, and when my brother come from the army after the war in the fall of '45, we spent that winter down there trapping and fishing. I had some hoop nets and we put out traps and stuff.

Anyway, we had a bunch of old wood around there we'd piled in the back room for kindling for the fireplace, and we'd bring possums home that we'd caught in the steel traps and just turn 'em aloose in the house. We had two little brown and black puppies about four or five months old, and they'd lay by that fireplace until I'd holler, "Sic him, get him!" and then they'd run out there and tree them possums up under that wood! People would come to visit and I'd tell 'em, "We's fixing to go possum hunting!" They'd look at me, you know, and I'd say, "It don't take long, we can catch a possum anytime. You can go possum hunting day or night." Then I'd holler, "Sic him, get him!" and them puppies would jump up and go out there and dig under that wood and tree. We'd move the wood around, and there he was, then turn him back aloose.

Later in the forties I went to work in the war plant, but I pretty much kept up my fishing and hunting. Another of my sidelines was finding lost articles in the lake. I did have some practice. For a long time I had hid nets and articles from the game warden and revenuers and could go back and find them pretty good. Sometimes I'd hide

them on such a dark night that I couldn't find 'em in the daytime; I'd
have to go back at night to find 'em. As time went on, people got to
losing things and dropping motors in the lake. One time I was visiting Mr. Franklin Jones, and he had real high-powered lawyers from
all over, including Mr. Bob Eckhardt from Houston, and he was telling 'em how good I was at finding things. Says, "He's real good. Truth
is, he sometimes finds things 'fore they're even lost."

I found one motor twice in the same week for Mr. Largent down
here on the river in about thirty feet of water. And once, there was
some boys lost a motor, and they knew exactly where it was but they
couldn't find it, so they told me where it was, but I went down about
a hundred yards there to another tree that looked kinda like the one
they was pointing at, and found their motor. Once I found eyeglasses
for a person who had lost 'em in the lake. He had hit a tree limb and
it threw 'em off. But, when I began to get earpieces and nosepieces,
he said, "No use finishing if it's in that many pieces!"

But anyway, along about twenty-five years ago there was an old
gentleman named Campbell from over in the oil fields who had retired and come down on the lake. He had got him a racing-type boat
made out of wood and a big monstrosity of a four-cylinder Evinrude
motor, and he was flying up and down the river and having a big
time. One day, up the river 'bout midway between Uncertain and the
park area, the back end of his boat come loose and this locomotive
motor went in the lake and carried the plow lines and the cable and
controls with it. But there was enough boat left that he and the fellow with him were able to float. I was working in the plant then on
evening shift, and this Mr. Campbell was headquartering out from
Crip's Camp. That evening Crip called me and told me about the
mishap and the motor in the lake. I didn't like them big motors
much anyway, but Crip says, "He's offering fifty dollars to find it."
"Well," I says, "that sounds like it'll be a good way to get it found." So
the next day I hunted till noon and didn't find it. The second day I
found it about eleven o'clock down on the river, and I was able to
pull it up off the bottom and work it towards the bank, and finally
get on the bank and drag it into shallow water, and get out waist deep
and roll it in the boat. I hate 'em anyhow!

So I brought it on up to Shine Hale's Camp and left it there on my
boat and came on up to the government pump station and called Crip's
Camp and told 'em I had the motor. Then Crip called Mr. Campbell,
and in an hour or so he called me at home, says, "Mr. Campbell's down
here. He says he won't pay fifty dollars for it. He'll just pay twenty-
five." "Well," I said, "I'll see what I can do." And I went back down

there on the river and threw the motor back overboard where it had been, near as I could guess.

Then I went on down to meet Mr. Campbell. He wanted to know where the motor was, and I told him I had put it back like it was 'fore it all started. Well, he kind of flared up a little bit, and I left pretty soon. I didn't feel I had made any headway. And when I got home, Crip called again and says, "Mr. Campbell's done got kinda hot. He may sue you." I got ready to go to work and got to the job, and pretty soon the phone rang. Mr. Campbell was in Marshall in Mr. Hale Eliot's office, who was then sheriff. Mr. Hale Eliot talked about what I'd done and said didn't I think that was a dirty trick? I said, "Well, yeah, might be, 'cause the old motor was dirty and when I threw it overboard I did rinse my hands off." He said, "I advise you to go back and get it." I told him I'd done had it once! He says, "Well, he may want to sue you." But I thought to myself, "I've done lost fifty dollars that day on it, if I went and got it again and didn't collect I'd be out a hundred."

So I waited a little bit, and they waited for me to say something, and finally Mr. Eliot wanted to know what I was gonna do. I asked him, "If y'all sue, how you gonna word the suit? How you gonna file?" He says, "We been talking to Philip Baldwin, the county attorney, and Philip says it would be kinda like a person that picked up a stray cow, and kept it awhile, and then turned it aloose and it got killed on the highway." I don't know whether Philip got that out of the *Southwestern Reporter* or not.

Well, that was their version, but I figured I was the only witness they had and I wouldn't make a very good witness for the prosecution. So I waited awhile and he admonished me again, was I gonna get it? I told him I don't believe I was, and it finally died on off. That was the last I heard of it, except about a month or two later there's a couple of boys come over around Karnack wanting to buy old wrecked outboards, or any old motors that wouldn't run. Said they come from Kilgore, but I believe Mr. Campbell had 'em over there as decoys.

So I worked in the plant for twenty-odd years until I retired, and the world went on. But like always I hunted and fished and watched the river and the lake. About midway between Jefferson and the State Park area, on the north side of the river, and some seven or eight miles from the nearest highway, is one Howard Miller, who drifted into this country forty years ago from up in Wood County. He's sort of a backwoodsman, sort of a nice old gentleman. A sawmill man up on the road taken a liking to him and told him to go down to the river if he wanted to and camp in one of the old houses that he had left when he had a sawmill down there, and sort of look after some hogs he had in the woods. So Howard went down to the river and he squatted in this old dilapidated house for a temporary period, which has lasted forty years.

I don't know just what kind of a deal Mr. Mauldlin at the sawmill made with Howard, but he claims that he's homesteaded a hundred-and-some-odd acres of land, and has leased or rented up and down the river to people from Gilmer and Gladewater and around—some trailer houses and a couple of permanent houses. Now there's one old man lawyer in Jefferson who's drifted in there, hasn't been there all his life, who is in the course of trying to claim Howard's land and evict him. I don't know the legal aspects, but there's public consternation against that.

Miller's a very interesting man to talk to—sorta bewhiskered, a very simple person who doesn't even know what's down the river at the dam. He just knows there where he is. At one time, he taken the authority to warn other fishermen not to fish gill nets up and down the river for a certain distance there. He decided he might hold a claim there, since nobody ever came along. I used to observe him as I went up the river in my motorboat. He'd come to the front of his cabin door and the edge of the riverbank, which is a short distance from his cabin door. The river has sorta high banks there, and the view from it didn't include his house.

But after he'd been there some twenty-five years he began to admonish the other fishermen that he had that area staked off. The game warden was informed and went up to discuss the matter with him—Mr. Ellis, a very diplomatic person, who wasn't trying to be hard on anybody. He went up to Howard's by boat and got there about nine o'clock in the morning. When he got out and went up to the house, Howard was already standing in the door, but he come out on the porch and pulled the door shut. Mr. Ellis begin to explain to him that he understood Howard had been warning other fishermen, and that he couldn't stake off an area like that. He could fish the whole lake hisself, and so could anybody else, properly licensed and so forth, with their nets.

At that time Howard still had a lot of hogs in the woods, and Mr. Ellis observed a bunch of little pigs a month or so old on the porch just squealing and running into you and taking on terrible! They couldn't hardly hear each other talk. Mr. Ellis didn't know what the pigs was concerned about till finally Howard, in desperation, just threw the door open and hollered, "Well, go get it then!" It was a two-room house, and the pigs rushed in the kitchen part, and under his eating table Howard had a half of a log hollered out and boards nailed over each end. He had poured the morning's feed for the pigs in this little trough and was letting them come in the house where the big old hogs couldn't beat 'em away from the feed. So, if that ain't a hermit I don't know where you gonna find one!

I only started visiting with Mr. Howard in the last six or seven years, but I was instrumental once in getting two movie people to film him with his fourteen dogs. Spent a half a day over there, and they put on a remarkable treatise on Mr. Howard Miller on Channel 13 TV News out of Shreveport. This dog picture was a remarkable picture where Howard paddled along the river and these dogs followed along the bank right beside him as long as they could see him in the boat.

But later I was over there and he didn't have any dogs. None. And he told me they was gone. He was a little reluctant about it, but he divulged enough of information that they had been running and killing deer, and he had decided to get rid of 'em. Some of his neighbors that comes down from Gilmer and him had taken 'em out in the woods and executed 'em! They started to save one, but Howard said he didn't think that would be fair because he liked all fourteen of 'em the same amount, and he hated to single one out and save him and let the others go. So he just let them all went.

Anyway, he doesn't have any hogs in the woods anymore. He gardens some, and he cuts his own wood with a little bucksaw. The deer eat up his garden. And he says if a hoot owl hollers in the middle of the day it's going to rain in so many hours. He did eat armadilloes quite a bit. He has since had his friends, who come and camp down the river from him, build him a pretty good little new two-room house between the old house and the river.

He would never invite anyone into his old house. You could see in the door, but you couldn't see very far, because it was a tunnel 'round in there between piles of I don't know what—old papers and this and that, trappers' supplies, coon hides, a wood-burning stove.

He's about seventy-three. He's smart in his ways, but he don't have the grasp of the earth completely. He makes you feel like that you wish that you was one of him.

I don't know what kind of a deal Mr. Mauldlin at the sawmill made with him forty years ago, probably nearly none, but this one old lawyer in Jefferson is trying to claim his land and evict him. There's a man in Jefferson who knows his business, a Mr. Haggard, and I intend to go see him today. Haggard and I have talked about seeing if Mr. [Frank] Tolbert of the *Dallas Morning News* wouldn't help out in the matter. I don't know, it's just a challenge that I want to take up and do something about. I might get whupped or shot at, but that's all right.

Well, it's night on Taylor Island, and I'm looking at the moon and waiting for the alligators to alligate and the hoot owls to hoot. It's a wonderful world, ain't it? It's a wonderful world for them people that is alive. I know a whole lots of people staggering around that is dead as hell, don't see nothing, been dead most of their lives. Some people never see a sunrise, or if they see it, never thought nothing about it. I think every sun that rises done it just for me.

Building the Last Caddo Bateau

Building the Last Caddo Bateau

*All my life I've fiddled with boats. I 'spect I've
built 180 to 200, all wood boats. I like wood.
A wood boat is much better for one's health
than a metal one. The vibrations of a metal
boat have a very adverse effect on a person's
central nervous system—causes headaches
and high blood pressure. Mother lived to be
over ninety years old, and she rode only in
wood boats. A wood boat absorbs vibration
and soothes one's nerves. Why, an outboard
will last two or three times longer on a wood
boat than a metal one. In hot weather, the
shade under a wood boat is cool. A metal
boat is hot and drives away fish. Besides, if a
metal boat fills with water, it sinks. A wood
boat floats.*

*But boat building is not like piling up some
brush. If you don't do it right you wind up
with something crooked.*

—WYATT A. MOORE

On Taylor Island, at nine o'clock Saturday
morning, June 28, 1983, Wyatt Moore and Paul
Ray Martin started with two shaped mulberry
stems, four 16' cypress boards, assorted pieces
of cypress planking, a sack full of nails, some
silicone caulking compound, and a crude blueprint sketched on a scrap of plywood. By three
o'clock that afternoon the boat was more or
less completed except for some minor finishing work, sanding, and painting. The following
day at about noon, after a special treatment to
seal and waterproof the hull, Moore officially
launched and successfully tested the craft on
the waters of Caddo Lake.

As Moore summed up the construction process, "We started on it on Saturday morning and rode in it on Sunday. We built the boat from scratch—there was nothing but lumber, just lumber laying out there. Wasn't anything but lumber sawed up."

Work began with the shaping of bow and stern stems from a log of mulberry. The ends of two 16′ × 1′ × ⅝″ cypress boards were cut to form bow and stern angles and then nailed to the mulberry stems to create the sides of the boat. Three large bulkheads, placed to create a live box for fish and a minnow well, gave the sides a graceful curve. Small cross supports or knees were placed about 15″ apart throughout the inside bottom of the boat for additional stiffening of the hull. Two other 16′ cypress boards were cut to fit diagonally across the bottom of the boat. Decking was fitted over the bow and stern, and partial decking was placed to frame the live box and minnow well. A lattice cover for the live box and a simple seat were made. Finally, the craft was painted a dark green, the traditional color for this kind of boat.

The boat design is that of Wyatt Moore, who throughout his long life has built wooden boats for use on Caddo Lake, mostly types referred to locally as "paddle skiffs" and "bateaux." These types are commonly called "esquifs" and "plank pirogues" in Arcadian Louisiana. Moore learned his boatbuilding techniques from Frank Galbraith, a near-legendary Caddo Lake boatbuilder. Perhaps the last living builder of this type of boat in the Caddo Lake area, Moore was ably assisted in the construction by his friend Paul Ray Martin, a skilled carpenter and builder of fiberglass kayaks.

In its heyday, the Caddo Lake bateau was noted for speed, maneuverability, and seaworthiness. The functional, canoe-like craft was widely used by fishermen, hunters, fishing guides, and bootleggers before the introduction of aluminum and fiberglass motorboats after World War II.

Moore recalls using his bateaux for a variety of activities, legal and illegal:

Once, nearly everybody felt that one of those little fishing boats was a necessity, not a luxury. You couldn't go out there and do a hard day's fishing in a big old hard-to-paddle boat, and get up in here, there, and yonder, and cover lots of territory and keep the fish alive. The old-time fishing boat was a tool of the trade, and was designed to serve that purpose. There was a couple here [on Taylor Island]. They each had a bateau and fished until they died.

I used to use one of 'em a good deal in the fall of the year. I would take a Buelspinner on a cane pole and troll the edge of the timber and hunt the squirrels out over the water, and fish in combination with it, and/or maybe kill a duck. I'd come in with ducks, squirrels, and a few fish, every day. I hauled a full-grown deer from up the creek in one, one day. And during the seven or eight years I almost exclusively made whiskey, I had a bateau I had carried eight hundred pounds of whiskey in. I knew they couldn't out-paddle me in a bateau boat, and I could go places where they couldn't go. Here, our method was mostly to put a platform out over the water in Caddo Lake in thickets where only a small canoe-like boat could get into, and run five or six barrels of mash. I never did plow one of Jim Ferguson's mules, but some of my friends of mine told me that they thought that I would finally make it. But I didn't quite.

Typically, in the 1930's, one of these boats would have sold for $35 to $40; the present reproduction costs about $100, excluding labor. In many ways this particular "folk boat" seems unique to the Caddo Lake area, perhaps evolving from the plank pirogue of southern Louisiana.

William B. Knipmeyer, in his classic study, "Folk Boats of Eastern French Louisiana," distinguished six kinds of Arcadian folk boats. These were the dugout pirogue, plank pirogue, chaland, esquif, flatboat, and bateau. The Arcadian "bateau," a large, flat-bottomed rowing boat with blunt bow and stern, is a very different craft from Moore's creation. Instead, his boat seems a special Caddo Lake variant of the plank pirogue, perhaps most closely resembling the plank pirogues of the Atchafalaya Basin. Describing the Atchafalaya pirogue at the time of his 1950 study, Knipmeyer noted, "In the Atchafalaya Basin, plank pirogues are smallest and have the most sheer. Generally they have a coaming about two inches wide at the waist, which diminishes to nothing toward the bow and stern. Often they are equipped with fish wells, which are made by placing two boards about two feet apart across the waist of the boat. Holes are bored in the bottom of the boat and closed with plugs."[1] As will be shown, the perforated fish box/bait well is a striking feature of Moore's Caddo Lake bateau.

The plank pirogue, perhaps the direct ancestor of the Caddo bateau, had developed around 1900 in southeastern Louisiana from the modern dugout pirogue, which was hewn from a single cypress log. As Knipmeyer observed, "The remarkable similarity between the dugout and the plank pirogues in form, size, use, and associated equipment makes it clear that the former was the inspiration for the latter. The time of the plank pirogue's arrival coincides with the expansion of cypress lumbering activities, which created new uses and a greater need for pirogues. It seems certain that these new interests did not invent the plank pirogue, but they were undoubtedly responsible for making it more popular and spreading its use."[2]

The modern form of the Arcadian dugout pirogue, the immediate ancestor of the plank pirogue, had itself evolved from an earlier and larger variety of Arcadian dugout. This large pirogue had been in wide use all across the southeastern United States, and derived in turn from aboriginal forms of the dugout. Native Americans used the bark canoe in the

---

1. William B. Knipmeyer, "Folk Boats of Eastern French Louisiana," in *American Folklife*, ed. Don Yoder (Austin: University of Texas Press, 1977), p. 130.

2. Ibid., p. 127.

North, bullboats in the West, dugouts on the West Coast, and the ancestral pirogue dugout in the Southeast.[3]

So, in both form and function, the Caddo bateau which Wyatt Moore and Paul Ray Martin assembled in the spring of 1983 seems a lineal descendant of the ancient Indian dugouts described by early French and British explorers in the Southeast. The intervening stages of "larger nineteenth-century dugout pirogue" and "modern dugout pirogue" may or may not have been present at Caddo Lake, but they were certainly present in Arcadian Louisiana. Moore's boat springs from a long tradition.

The pattern for this particular form of the Caddo Lake version of the plank pirogue was taken from a surviving boat built by master builder Frank Galbraith. Galbraith lived with Moore for several years in the 1920's and strongly influenced his boat designs and construction techniques. Galbraith, according to Moore, was "the Cadillac of the industry."

Galbraith's tombstone has written on it, "A builder of fine boats." He was a marvelous man with tools. If he wanted to make something to do something with, he'd just whittle it out and make it. He could almost look at a place he wanted to put a piece of timber and saw it to fit. He'd saw it a little bit long to start with and then he'd put it down in there and scribe it, mark on either side of it, and then he'd saw it out. He said he never used a rule much; he could guess it better. But he could twist that wood around and do a marvelous job of working! He was a very conscientious worker who wouldn't put a piece of poor material in a boat. He said there wasn't no use in wasting that much labor with poor material. He wouldn't use anything but the best red heart cypress lumber.

Although Galbraith built some bateaux for himself and for his friends, his specialty was larger, much more complicated wooden boats,

---

3. Ibid., p. 108.

especially large inboard motorboats. Large or small, all of Galbraith's boats showed his genius for innovative design and his skill with wood. Galbraith-designed boats were almost all characterized by a high degree of "twist" in their side boards, giving them a high degree of "flair" in the sides.[4] Moore describes these design characteristics.

He built an awful good skiff, an eighteen-foot-long pulling boat. I built skiffs just like his later. He would take eighteen-inch boards and nail them to a stem and kind of flair them out at the front and come on back with them flaired out and put a back end in them. They were sort of **V**-*bottomed. When they were lightly loaded, they floated up pretty high and you could get in 'em with oars and go pretty good with them. But, as you began to load 'em, because of the fact that they were flaired out at about a forty-five degree angle, they immediately increased their lifting power.*

The flair we put in the side of our boat was characteristic of a Galbraith boat. In sixteen feet, we put an almost complete twist in 'em. Frank could build any kind little something out of wood that he'd envisioned. He'd make that wood do it! He told me he would lay in the bed at night and figure out every inch of an inboard motorboat—how long the engine was, and where he was gonna set it in the boat, and how much propeller shaft he needed, and all—then he'd build it.

Knipmeyer mentions that the terms "two-plank pirogue" and "three-plank pirogue," referring to the number of planks in the bottom, were in general use in Arcadian Louisiana at the time of his 1950 study. These terms were both descriptive and expressions of value. A two-plank pirogue had two planks in its bottom, a three-plank pirogue had three, and the

---

4. "Flare" is a term used to describe a hull cross-section that grows increasingly wider as it rises from the waterline toward the tops of the sides.

fewer seams, the better.[5] The fewer seams in
the bottom, the fewer places there were to
leak. All other things being equal, a two-plank
pirogue was more trouble-free and more valuable than a three-plank model. Moore doesn't
use these terms, though he gives clear indica-
tion he shares the opinion that the fewer
planks in the bottom, the better the boat. In
fact, he suggests as explanation for the narrow
beam of the Galbraith boat that Galbraith had
designed this type of bateau to have only one
cypress board on its bottom—to be in effect a
"one-plank pirogue."

*Galbraith used to, in his standard bateau
building, order two 12" pieces 16' long and
one 20" piece 16' long, and he'd put that 20"
piece on the bottom. Therefore, he'd make
the inside of the boat about 18½" wide, and
then that one 20" piece'd cover the bottom. A
boat that cocks up at each end, if your seam
goes down the front, in the hot summertime
it'll open up when you're not using it. [Then]
if you get in and start using it, that bottom
loads and that front goes down and you'll
have a leak. Galbraith recognized that. It's
the reason he put 'em crossways and/or used
a solid bottom.*

THE BLUEPRINT

Moore's "blueprint" for the bateau consists of a
scrap of plywood with only the basic dimensions—overall length of the boat, location of
the bulkheads, taper and size of the bulkheads,
and bow and stern angles—noted upon it
(Fig. 1). He took these measurements from a
surviving Galbraith bateau owned by Mr. Miller
of the Leigh Community, near Karnack, Texas.
Moore describes this process and indicates the
procedure he would have used had no boat been
available from which to take a pattern.

*Did you notice that piece of plywood there at
Martin's house that we would lay this bevel*

5. Knipmeyer, "Folk Boats of Eastern French Louisiana," pp. 127–128.

square on now and then, and set it? Well, that stems from the fact that when we were down at this other boat we would lay the bevel square in that boat that Galbraith built and take the angles of them bulkheads. Then we would lay the square up over this piece of plywood and put that angle back on record. Then we could go back to it with the bevel square and pick it up and apply it to the boat. That's the reason we moved along as fast as we did, 'cause I had premeditated that deal and could safely go ahead and cut the bulkheads without thinking on 'em. Ordinarily, if I hadn't of had the pattern, I would have bended the [side] boards around and put some false braces in there and clamped it and sorta looked at it endways and sideways. Then, if it suited me, I'd have measured the width and the angle and then cut the bulkheads and put 'em in to fit that particular boat.

Moore, who once had a whole shop full of plywood boards with patterns on them, used these as a general guide, improvising and modifying where necessary.

People coming in for me to build them one could look at another boat and say, "Well, I'd like mine a little wider or a little this or a

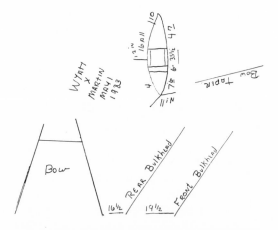

FIGURE I.
Blueprint.

FIGURE I *drawn by Wyatt Moore; all others drawn by James H. Conrad*

*little that." Then I could put a bevel square
in there and take a pattern off it and go ahead
and make slight alterations on it. If a fellow
wanted a boat I'd get hold of my blueprints
and sort of build it to whatever purpose he
wanted it. But if I wanted to slightly change
it, I would. I'd have the board hanging up in
the shop. Maybe I would use that board later
to make a boat of it.*

WOODS

Like Frank Galbraith before him, Moore uses
only good red heart cypress from Louisiana
and native mulberry wood: cypress for the side
boards, bottom, bulkheads, cross supports, and
decking, and mulberry for the stems and stem
guards. He calls the heart cypress and mulberry "woods eternal," and argues that red cypress will last longer than pine or native white
cypress, and will stand twisting better and
more easily than other woods. He observes
that some white cypress bateaux he has seen
on the lake rotted within four or five years,
while bateaux built from red cypress lasted
twenty-five to thirty years if properly maintained. In his opinion, "To build out of native
[white] cypress, with the differences in the
length of time that it would last and the
amount of work that would go into it, a good
high-priced red cypress boat is the cheapest in
the long run, by far."

TOOLS

Moore has a somewhat ambivalent attitude toward modern power tools used for boatbuilding. He much prefers hand tools—hand saw,
hand plane, hatchet, etc.—when working by
himself, but he clearly sees the convenience
and speed of power tools. During the building
of the bateau, he seemed to delight in Martin's
skilled use of them.

Moore's assistant Paul Ray Martin, a professional carpenter and contractor, has no qualms
about the new tools, using them with all the
speed, certainty, and nonchalance Moore had

earlier ascribed to Frank Galbraith.[6] Early in the construction, a pattern was established. Moore would begin an item of work by hand, and Martin would finish it off with his power tools. It was Martin who introduced the modern innovations of silicone caulking compound, cement-covered nails, and cement sealers to the traditional process of bateau construction.[7]

SHAPING THE MULBERRY STEMS

The first step in boat construction is the preparation of the mulberry stems for the bow and stern pieces (Fig. 2). Moore saws a 4' length off a log of mulberry and then splits it with an axe and sledgehammer into wedge-shaped sections. For the roughing out and trimming of the stems, he uses a hatchet; for finishing and dressing off, he uses a hand plane, bevel, and square. To flatten and angle the stem, he cuts off the back of the piece of mulberry, flattens it with a plane, lays two squares on it to be sure that it is flat and true, establishes a centerline through the stem, and places a bevel at the top and bottom to determine the flair. The secret of preparing the stem, according to Moore, is to leave the top a little wider and a little more flaired than the bottom of the stem. Since the side boards will nail directly to the bow and stern stems, the shape of the stems plays a

MULBERRY STEM

STEM GUARD

MULBERRY LOG

FIGURE 2.
Stem and guard.

---

6. Moore and Martin soon established a pattern for working together that they followed throughout the boat construction. Moore would begin a unit of work with his hand tools, and Martin would finish it with his electric power tools. Most of the actual sawing and nailing, etc., was done by Martin under the direct supervision of Moore. To avoid confusion of names, we have prepared this narrative using Moore as the sole active agent in the construction process. The exception to this rule is where Martin introduced an innovation to the boatbuilding, such as the use of silicone caulking to seal the seams.

7. Moore thinks that nails are superior to screws for boatbuilding purposes. Screws, he argues, take longer to put into a boat and, if you do not get the hole just right, can pull loose.

The first step in construction of the bateau is the cutting of the mulberry stems. Moore makes the top of the stem wider and with more flare.

critical role in determining the shape of the boat itself. As Moore explains this, "If you don't bring in the flair at the bottom [of the stem] to less pitch, the bottom of the boat will rear out too much and look dumpy." (Two more pieces of mulberry must be made to serve as stem guards, but these are added only when construction is almost over.)

SELECTING AND CUTTING THE SIDE BOARDS

Moore considers the selection of the two 16' cypress boards for the sides of the boat to be the most crucial step in the boatbuilding process. He says, "The decisions you make now will be with you for the rest of the construction." He carefully inspects the four cypress planks for size, flexibility, shape, and location

The two side boards, cut to the proper bow and stern angles, are examined. A 4" strip has been cut off the top ends of each board to keep bow and stern from sticking up too much.

of knotholes. The first side board, which becomes the pattern for the second side board, should be somewhat smaller than the other board so that the second board can be cut to fit. The two boards should be about matched in flexibility as well, and Moore bends the boards repeatedly to determine this. Regarding the sizing of the boards, Moore notes, "You got to start and figure your lumber and not cut your pattern from a board that is larger than the other boards. Preferably you should have boards of the same thickness and size to start with. What you need to do is make the [side] pattern out of the narrowest board you have."

Moore consults the blueprint board to determine the exact angle for the vertical line of bow and stern (which are the same). He places a bevel on the blueprint, gets the angle, and scribes it off on one end of the first side board, then trims the board on that line (Fig. 3). The process is repeated on the other end of the side board. The bottom and top of the side board are chosen on the basis of location of knotholes, with any knotholes that might occur placed toward the top.

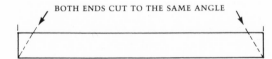

BOTH ENDS CUT TO THE SAME ANGLE

FIGURE 3.
Side board.

After nailing the board to sawhorses, Moore does some fine-tuning of its shape. Laying a flexible strip of wood along the top of the front one-third of the board, he scribes a shallow curved angle that is deepest at the bow and shallowest about 5'4" toward the center of the board (Fig. 4). This long, wedge-shaped sliver of side board is then trimmed off. The other end of the board is done in exactly the same way and the two cuts smoothed off with a plane.

FIGURE 4.
Bow and stern tapers.

The purposes here are both aesthetic and functional, as Moore notes: "What you do is to take off a little at both ends at the top because the boards are going to stick up and the sides are going to lean down, and if you don't take off some, the ends stick up too high in proportion to the bottom. Sometimes you cut some out of the bottom, a little strip from the bottom, if the boards don't have a little swoop to them." This fine-tuning of the pattern side board is of great importance to the ultimate shape and performance of the boat, and Moore sums up the considerations involved:

If you bend two boards around that are straight to make a boat, more than apt it will cock up too much at the ends. It's customary to set you a nail in your board about midway, or maybe a little bit from midway—to tack you a nail if your board is straight. Then you bend you a long strip from each end, taper out at each end, around this nail, and mark it, and cut you a kind of slight semicircle out of the bottom. If you don't, when you bend the boards over the bottom won't be straight enough, it'll rare up with too much rake. The reason I didn't cut any out of the bottom of [our pattern side board] was because I used as a pattern a board that already was crooked in the bottom. You noticed I put that curve [toward] the bottom! We had about a ³⁄₄" curve in the bottom of the original pattern to start with. I can almost look at a board which I'm gonna use and see the boat 'fore I even build it, what it's gonna look like, I've looked at so many. You either know or you don't know.

The pattern side board is now fully prepared. Moore carefully compares each of the remaining 16' cypress boards by placing them on the pattern board to see which one is the best possible fit in size and flexibility. After choosing one of them, he cuts the same end angles from the second board as from the first, and trims off the upper edges as before. Then, nailing the two side boards together, he carefully uses hand plane and draw knife to make them exactly alike. The sides of the bateau are now prepared.

CUTTING THE FIRST BULKHEAD

The front central bulkhead will determine the shape and curve of the boat, and the decision about its dimensions is the second most critical point in the construction process. The wider the angle and/or the greater the width of the bulkheads, the greater the carrying capacity of the boat. (Width of the front central bulkhead directly determines width of the boat, since the flexible side boards will be bowed to fit the bulkhead. Likewise, the side angles of the bulkhead determine the flair of the boat's sides once the flexible sides are nailed in place. The two factors of width and degree of flair are most important in determining carrying capacity.)

Moore likes to cut all three bulkheads from the same piece of board to save wood and to insure uniformity. The little pieces of scrap wood left over from making the bulkheads will come in handy later for cross supports and decking. Wood is valuable, and, as Moore says, "It's like rendering lard from a hog, you can use it all if you watch."

Following the directions on the blueprint, the front central bulkhead should measure 30½" at the widest end and 19½" at the narrowest.[8] Moore saws this bulkhead, but waits on the others to custom fit them after the first bulkhead has been nailed into place (Fig. 5).

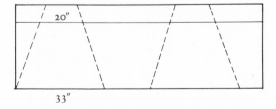

FIGURE 5.
Pattern for bulkheads.

8. Construction of the boat is done with bottom up until the latter stages. Only after the bottom has been fitted is the boat turned right side up.

Before deciding on the exact locations of the bulkheads, Moore first measures the overall length of the side boards. After deciding that the front central bulkhead will go 7'5" from the bow, the rear bulkhead 3'9" from the front central one, and the back central bulkhead 6" from the front central one, [9] he clamps the two side boards together and scribes the location of the bulkheads inside and out (Fig. 6). At the same time, the mulberry stems are laid on the bow and stern of the side boards and scribed inside and out. The clamps are then removed.

Before moving on to nail the side boards onto the mulberry stems, Moore checks the flair of the sides by placing some small pieces of wood on the stems and seeing how they angle out (Fig. 7). This is something of a last precaution before bending the side boards. The basic rule of thumb is that the shorter the boat, the less twist a side board will stand.

FIGURE 6.
Location of bulkheads and stems.

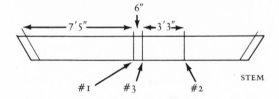

FIGURE 7.
Checking the flair of the sides.

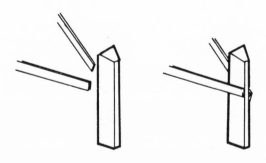

9. Moore has made slight adjustments from the blueprint measurements taken from Galbraith's boat. Spacing of the bulkheads is based on the overall length of the boat. Moore does not seem to have a mathematical formula, but he takes into consideration the weight distribution in the water. Move the

NAILING THE SIDE BOARDS
TO THE BOW AND STERN STEMS

Moore lays one of the side boards on the ground, places a stem under one end with about 3″ sticking out above and below the board, and nails it to the outer edge (Fig. 8). Only the outer edge is nailed at this time, since once the boards have been warped around the bulkhead, any nails on the inner edge would tend to pull out. The board is turned upright and the second side board placed against the front stem and nailed to it. According to Moore, it is vital for the two boards to be at the same height on the stem. This is best achieved by placing lumber under the ends of the two boards that are being nailed together (Fig. 9). The stern stem is then nailed to one of the side boards at the other end.

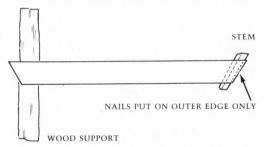

STEM

NAILS PUT ON OUTER EDGE ONLY

WOOD SUPPORT

FIGURE 8.
Nailing first side board to stem.

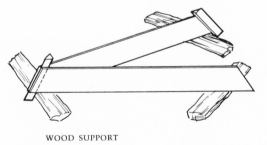

WOOD SUPPORT

FIGURE 9.
Nailing side boards to stems.

first bulkhead too far toward the stern, and the weight of the paddler and the water in the minnow well/live box will cause the bow to ride too high in the water; move the first bulkhead too far forward and the boat's stern will stick up in the air.

Moore and Martin nail the two side boards together at the stems. A 3' strip of wood (slightly wider than the bulkhead) holds the sides apart for the insertion of the first bulkhead.

BENDING THE SIDE BOARDS TOGETHER AROUND THE FIRST BULKHEAD

For nailing the open ends together, Moore inserts a temporary divider board (slightly wider than the bulkhead) about halfway along the two side boards. He then slowly and cautiously brings the two open side boards together and nails them at the stern stem. Again, only the outer edges of the side boards are nailed to the stem (Fig. 10). This operation takes at least two persons to perform successfully. After this, Moore suggests that "it won't hurt that lumber to sit there a minute and get used to itself."

Moore then proceeds to build a special rig to bend the boards around the first bulkhead. Two 4' strips of lumber are anchored with C-clamps to the side boards next to where the bulkhead is to be placed. Then nails are driven into the tops of these bending boards and a rope secured between them (Fig. 11). After dropping the bulkhead into place, Moore removes the temporary divider board keeping the two sides apart and adjusts the bottom of the bulkhead until it is level and square with the bottom of the side boards (remember, the boat is upside down!). The two bending boards are gradually brought together, twisting the side boards into a tight position against the bulkhead, and fastened in that position with the rope. "You don't want to bend it all in a moment," Moore

FIGURE 10.
Bending side boards.

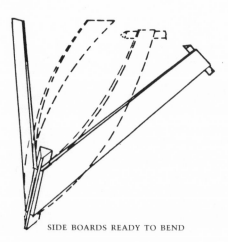

SIDE BOARDS READY TO BEND

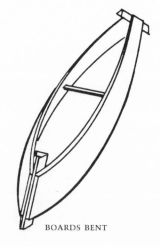

BOARDS BENT

cautions at this point. "It might have a fit." Then nails are driven into the sides to secure the bulkhead in place. (Cement-covered nails are used to hold the bulkhead to the sides, since these are less likely to pull out under stress than finishing nails, which will be used elsewhere.) After nailing the bulkhead, Moore slacks tension on the bending boards, first securing the bow and stern with C-clamps to keep them from popping loose under the strain (Fig. 12). Moore comments on the bending of the sides and other matters:

It doesn't look like those cypress planks would bend like that. It has quite a bend to it. I attempted to build one to my Dad's specifications once, and he kept wanting it a little wider in the back, and I knew he oughtn't to have it. I was trying to curve it out farther and it busted loose and split the whole side out. He and I roped it back in place and nailed it with a panel inside and it went on until it rotted. It always had a brand on it that you could recognize.

At this point, Moore places the boat, still bottom up, on sawhorses, and checks the alignment by stretching a string from one end of the boat to the other. This string goes right down the center of the boat from stem to stem and allows Moore to check the symmetry and pitch of the sides. The sides on the right and left of the string divider seem perfectly equal. Although nothing particular is said about it, Moore, Martin, and onlookers breathe a collective sigh of relief. The most treacherous stages in the process of bateau-construction have been successfully completed.

Moore bends the side boards around the front central bulkhead.

FIGURE 11.
Bending board C-clamped to sides; bulkhead on ground.

FIGURE 12.
C-clamps on stems.

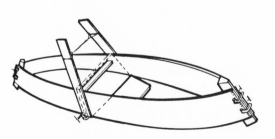

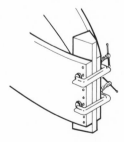

After the side boards have been nailed around the first bulkhead, the boat is placed bottom up on level sawhorses and a string is stretched down the center of the boat from stem to stem. The string allows Moore to check the bateau's symmetry.

It will be essential from now on that the sawhorses be kept absolutely level lest the boat end up twisted. As Moore observes,

You take the boat off them [the sawhorses] and look across them and see if they are equal. It don't matter if they're level so long as they have the same pitch. There ain't no use in doing anything more on the boat until the horses are level. You can look down them and see if they are alike—look across them and see if one is higher than the other. No need to try it setting on an illegal foundation.

PLACEMENT OF THE SECOND AND THIRD BULKHEADS

The sides were made to fit the first bulkhead, and that bulkhead determined the shape, flair, and "rocker" of the boat.[10] Now, with the second and third bulkheads, the bulkheads must be made to fit the sides of the boat. Moore custom cuts the second and third bulkheads to fit the curve and shape of the side boards, although the sides can be moved slightly to accommodate the new bulkheads. Moore explains the intricacies of placement and shape of the bulkheads as they relate to the performance of the boat:

After you put in one bulkhead, you put the others wherever the bulkhead lay; or, if you want to spread it a little, you could put it out a little. You can generally look at it. You don't want it to come out here and then sway in and come back again. After you bend it around and then look at it, the more you flair it, the more you can rare it up. That one has got exactly the right bend because your weight is going to be up where it is kind of wide. The back end tends to hang down somewhat. If you had the front end real sharp and the back end wide, then you have got to put an awful lot of ballast in it to keep it from running bow-heavy. Now, the one I

---

10. "Rocker" is the upward curvature of the keel line from the center toward the ends of the boat.

busted for my Dad, I built it to suit him, but it wasn't right; it was too wide in behind and it was always front-heavy. If it is too wide up there, you can't reach over and paddle properly.

The angle and width of the sides are checked by Moore with bevel and square, and each of the two remaining bulkheads cut to fit. In fitting the bulkheads into the boat, Moore's rule is to work to the angle that has the most flair. Otherwise, the boat will tend to twist itself out of shape with the addition of each new bulkhead and cross support. Again, the bulkheads must be level and square with the top and bottom of the sides. The front central bulkhead, the one forming the forward wall of the minnow well, went in first, now followed by the second, which forms the back wall of the live box, and the third, the one between the minnow well and the live box. Cement-covered nails are used to nail the second and third bulkheads in place.

Martin fits the second bulkhead, which will become the stern wall of the built-in fish box. The second and third bulkheads are "custom fitted" to the first.

After placement of the second bulkhead, Moore removes the bending boards from amidships and the C-clamps from bow and stern before nailing the third bulkhead. Additional lines of nails now are driven into bow and stern stems. To Martin's question "How many nails?" Moore replies, "Nail the hell out of it!" A remarkable number of nails are so placed. According to Moore, only the dense mulberry wood will take this abuse without splitting.

PLACEMENT OF CROSS SUPPORTS

Moore makes the cross supports, or "knees," out of 3" wide surplus cypress left over from the board used to cut the bulkheads. He determines the location of the supports by using the bulkheads as spacing guides, with the cross supports being placed about 15" apart down the bottom of the boat (Fig. 13). Moore advises, "Build the longer supports first and if you botch up one you can use it for the short cross pieces."

He measures the length of each support by laying it directly across the sides and marking the underside with a pencil. For the angle, he sets the support upright on the sides and puts the bevel on top of the support and measures the angle of the side. Then the support is set flat and the angle marked on it (Fig. 14). As with the bulkheads, he uses the side with the most pitch for the angle of both sides, noting, "If you keep giving to it, it will twist itself and turn wrong side out. You have to argue with it all the way." Finishing nails are used to nail the supports into the sides.[11] The bottom stems (only) are now cut flush with the sides (Fig. 15).

Moore measures a knee (cross support) to the bottom.

11. Galbraith laid his cross supports down flat in the boat. Moore explains why Galbraith did this, as well as why he chooses not to follow his old mentor on this minor point: "If you noticed [in the old Galbraith-made boat] he had some in the back stand-

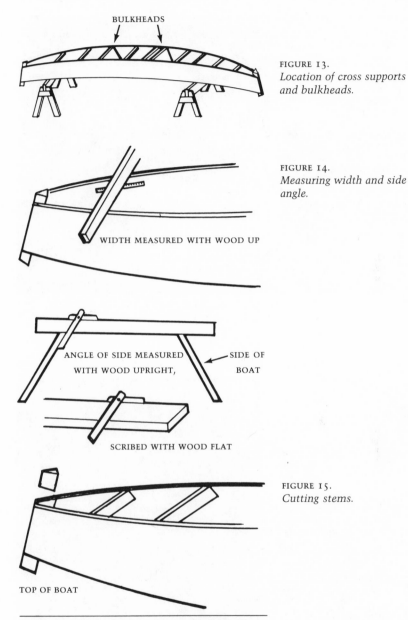

BULKHEADS

FIGURE 13.
*Location of cross supports
and bulkheads.*

FIGURE 14.
*Measuring width and side
angle.*

WIDTH MEASURED WITH WOOD UP

ANGLE OF SIDE MEASURED   SIDE OF
WITH WOOD UPRIGHT,   BOAT

SCRIBED WITH WOOD FLAT

FIGURE 15.
Cutting stems.

TOP OF BOAT

ing up, but there where the man set he didn't like to
have that high thing interfere with his feet all day
long. But when you put them cross supports flat in
there, they aren't very strong up and down, and the
nails go through [the cross supports laid down flat],
so you have to clinch them and they come loose."

Moore uses a modified bread scraper to "rough smooth" the edges of the side boards before planing.

Martin and Moore plane the knees and side boards smooth for the bottom boards.

FITTING THE BOTTOM

As necessary preparation, Moore planes the bottom of the bulkheads, the side boards, and the cross supports level and flat. This is quite an operation to work down by hand, but all must be absolutely flush with the side boards before the bottom can be put on the boat. Moore has modified an old bread scraper (Fig. 16) to use to work down the sides; a draw knife will not work because one's hands tend to hit the cross ribs when the knife is drawn across the side boards.

FIGURE 16.
Modified bread scraper.

The boat is now ready for the bottom boards—the remaining two 16' cypress planks. Following Frank Galbraith's practice, Moore sets the boards at a slight angle to the true center (Fig. 17), which allows the end seams to re-

FIGURE 17.
Bottom boards.

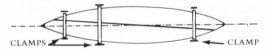

VIEW OF BOTTOM BOARDS AND CLAMPS

main in the water when the boat is beached, this keeping them swollen shut. Moore elaborates on this trick of the trade:

That crack won't be at the front where the boat sticks out of the water sometimes, and the crack will open up, and when you put the boat in the water, water will come into the boat. Putting the bottom boards at an angle is to avoid having the crack in front. The crack will be in the water where it will stay swelled up. Galbraith recognized that; it's the reason he put 'em on crossways, or used a solid bottom.

To insure that the boards completely cover the bottom, Moore places them side by side on the boat, measures and inspects them carefully, and scribes them, but only one bottom board will be cut at a time. Before nailing the first board to the bottom, he caulks the juncture between side boards and bottom board with space-age silicone, a long-lasting, flexible caulking compound suggested by Martin. Sil-

Following a practice of legendary boatbuilder Frank Galbraith, Moore and Martin place the two bottom boards at a slight angle to the true centerline of the boat.

icone will eventually be applied to all the
seams of the boat as permanent waterproofing.
In earlier days, Caddo Lake boatbuilders like
Moore and Galbraith did not use any kind of
caulking for their seams, relying instead upon
a heavy application of green paint at these
critical points and the natural tightening of
board-to-board junctures after soaking in
water. Moore describes this process:

We didn't use to use any caulking, but pre-
pared everything and took good oil-based
paint and just paint the bottom of the boat
good. Paint between the bottom and sides
and ribs and live box and everything, and
give it a good smearing of paint. You'd have
your bottom boards laying there, and paint
them real good and nail them down while
they're still wet, and that heavy paint under
there made a pretty good sealer. The crack
generally was so closely fitted that, if it
leaked a wee bit when you first put it in the
water, then overnight it would swell up, espe-
cially if the water was warm. If it was cold
wintertime, it would take a little longer to
swell up.

One of Moore's contemporaries helped this
process along by forcing a piece of twine down
the crack between bottom boards before painting. Another technique used by some boatbuilders was to stand one of the bottom boards
on edge and use some kind of blunt tool to
press one side of the board's edge out, to
"pooch it," as Moore says. This "pooched"
edge was then planed level before the boards
were joined on the bottom of the boat. The
bruising of the cypress would cause it to swell
more than would be the case normally, thus
better sealing the seam.

The last bottom board is now cut to fit.
Moore puts more silicone caulking on the upper edges of side boards, bulkheads, and cross
supports before pressing the second bottom
board in place. Furniture clamps are placed at
both ends and in the middle to squeeze the
bottom boards tightly together before nailing.
Moore nails from the center out, so that the

boards will not "crawl on him."[12] Finally, the bottom edges where side boards and bottom boards meet are planed and sanded and the seams caulked with silicone. Moore then turns the boat over for the first time in the boatbuilding process and planes the bulkheads flush with the sides.

The boat is briefly turned right side up for examination and to plane bulkheads flush with sides.

FITTING THE SKEG

Fitting the skeg requires the boat to be turned upside down again. The skeg, or "skag," as Moore terms it, is a 3' stabilizing fin, which is placed at the bateau's stern to help the rocker-bottomed craft track in a straight line. Cut from one of the remaining pieces of cypress

---

12. Ideally, the bottom boards should be a little thinner than the side boards, because it is difficult, according to Moore, to nail two boards together on the edge where one is as thick as the other.

scrap, the skeg is 3″ high at the back and tapers off toward the bow (Fig. 18). It is attached to the bottom of the boat about 2′ forward of the stern stem. Moore has an unusual way of nailing the skeg to the bottom. He puts the skeg where he wants it to go and scribes completely around it, removes the skeg, drives three nails within the scribed area, and then removes the nails. The nail holes serve as guides for permanently nailing the skeg from the inside of the boat. The skeg is placed back on the scribed area and temporarily nailed in place at each end. The boat is turned right side up and permanent nails driven home from inside. The temporary bottom nails are then removed.

The skeg was optional on the bateaux and skiffs built for Caddo Lake, but Moore almost always put them on his boats, since they stabilized a boat in high waves and kept it running straight under paddle. The skeg, along with the high degree of side flair and bottom rocker, made the Caddo Lake bateau a remarkably seaworthy craft, considering its small size. According to Moore,

I never knew of anybody getting drowned in one of the things. They respected 'em more, I guess. Down on the Big Lake, at Jeems Bayou, which comes in from the north, it's

SKEG

FIGURE 18.
Location of skeg.

BOW

Moore and Martin scribe the position of the skeg prior to nailing it from the inside of the boat.

*about a mile wide. The north wind sweeps
down through there, and I have heard somebody way back yonder talking about some
fellow come across there in one of 'em one
day, and part of the time you couldn't see
him, 'cause the waves was so high. Course,
one man in an empty boat, he'd probably set
down low in the bottom and it'd withstand a
lot of waves.*

Skegs were also placed on rowing skiffs.
Moore relates, "When we got to running motors
on the skiffs, we quit putting skags on the
boat. But before, when we pulled the boat with
oars, why we would put a little skag on it
that helped to hold the boat straight while
pulling it."

DECKING THE BATEAU

Moore likes to deck the bow, stern, live box,
and minnow well with surplus cypress. To hold
the cover (or decking) on the live box and minnow well, he nails a 3″ strip of wood to each
side, carefully fitting it to match the curve of
the boat's sides (Fig. 19). A lattice is then constructed to fit over the live box to keep fish
from jumping out (Fig. 20).

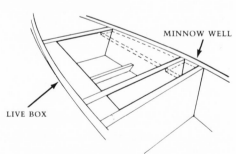

MINNOW WELL

LIVE BOX

FIGURE 19.
*Decking for live box, min-
now well, and bow and
stern.*

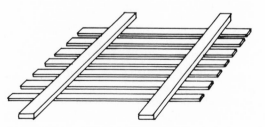

FIGURE 20.
Lattice for live box.

The live box and minnow well, which are located just aft of amidships, have holes bored in their bottoms or sides so that they exchange water with the lake or river to keep fish alive. Moore remarks on the utilitarian value of this remarkable live-box/minnow-well system:

If this was put into use by an old fisherman, he would drill some holes in the side where the minnows would stay alive. The minnow well would always carry water, and the live box would have four holes in the bottom or four holes in the side of the boat, and corks in them or wooden pegs that had been turned on a lathe. If you had fished all day, you might have thirty or forty fish in the live box, and it would carry water way on up in it and keep the fish alive. When you would have to pick up the fish to throw them in an [outside] live box to keep them for fish delivery day, you could hardly get the fish out without bailing out some water. You didn't have a dip net, usually didn't, so you would peg it up and bail it down low and clean it out and leave the pegs in. The next day, when you begin to catch a few fish, take the pegs out.

The weight of water in minnow well and live box is designed to balance with the weight of the paddler, who sits in an unusual position just forward of the midline of the boat. Single paddlers in pirogues normally sit toward the stern. Since the bateau's seat is placed to balance with minnow well and live box full of water, this means that when the bateau is paddled "dry," something must be added to the stern to trim the craft dead level. That something—and most unusual in a small paddle boat like this—is ballast (plastic milk jugs full of water). As Moore tells it,

If you don't carry water in the live box or some sort of ballast, the boat's stern will stick out of the water and will not be balanced properly in the water. If you move back toward the rear of the boat to balance it, you will be much too far back to paddle good. It was customary to place ballast in the

*end of the boat as well as have water in the
live box. If you don't carry ballast and set far
enough back to balance the boat, you would
be too far forward to paddle good. I usually
carry a good deal of ballast and put my seat
forward so that I can paddle good.*

Decking of stern and bow is done also with
surplus pieces of cypress. Moore cuts and fits
them, but they are not nailed into place until
the boat is painted. The stem guards are now
added, and holes for bow and stern lines are
drilled at a slight downward angle into the portions of the bow and stern stems which pro-
trude above the tops of the boat's sides (Fig. 21).

FIGURE 21.
*Mulberry guard for bow and
stern.*

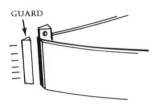

*Holes are drilled at a slight
downward angle into the
mulberry bow and stern
stems for rope holes. At this
stage in the boat construction, Moore puts decking at
the stems and around the
minnow well and live box.*

Bow stem after drilling.

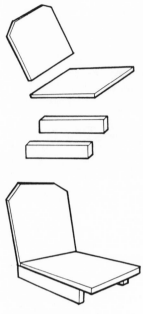

CONSTRUCTING THE SEAT

Moore makes the seat out of two 1" × 4" strips of cypress and two 2' × 2' cypress boards (Fig. 22). The seat support strips are cut about 14" long to fit snugly between the first bulkhead and the first cross support forward of the first bulkhead. Moore nails one of the boards at a slight angle to the seat supports to form the back of the seat, then decks them with the second board to form the seat's bottom.

The seat does not move around because it is jam-fitted between bulkhead and cross support, but it is not nailed into place. Consequently, as Moore notes, it can be moved about to fit special circumstances. As he and Galbraith would travel to their fishing grounds,

We would turn around and paddle backwards with the live box in front until we got there—just for traveling purposes—and then turn around and fish. Probably not paddle it back home backwards with the live box full of water and fish, because that wouldn't be practical.

FIGURE 22.
Seat for bateau.

Although Galbraith and other boatbuilders made such seats, and Moore placed one in this boat, he says that he seldom used such a seat himself, since he considered them bothersome, preferring instead some kind of more informal arrangement. As he says,

I never did like a seat because, when I wasn't fishing, I was making whiskey, and I would sometimes want to sit in the extreme end of a boat. I used a box and a cushion, or just a box. I had a wooden box, a .22 rifle ammunition box, that I picked up in Idabell, Oklahoma, one time. I used it for a seat, kept my rubber hose and funnel under it, and used it to pick up fish at the lake and carry 'em to the house and cut 'em up on the back [of the box] and eat 'em and then carry it back to the lake the next morning.

PAINTING AND MAINTENANCE

Now that all carpentry work is completed, Moore treats the bottom of the bateau with a cement sealer, an innovation suggested by Paul Ray Martin. The cement sealer, a temporary measure, is normally used to keep water out of cement until it can cure, but in this case it serves to keep moisture out of the boat until the boat is painted. After some days have passed, the whole boat is painted with two coats of meadow green lead-based paint. Moore tells the story of the farmer who had a wagon built, and the wagon builder asked him what color he wanted the wagon painted, and the farmer replied, "Any color as long as it is red." As Knipmeyer noted thirty-five years ago, the color of the pirogue (bateau) is invariably dark green.

Since cypress is a "wood eternal," not much maintenance was needed by the Caddo Lake bateaux like this one:

Well, the old way they were done was to build them and put them in the water and the water would swell up the seams. Paint it twice [to begin with], and about once a year you would scrape the scum off of the bottom of the boat and paint it or not repaint it. If it was built out of good lumber like those built by Galbraith, they'd last for twenty to twenty-five years before it rotted.

PADDLING THE BATEAU

For paddling the Caddo Lake bateau, Moore recommends a fairly short paddle, about 4'8" in length. In a paddle technique very different from that of the Cajun pirogue-men studied by Knipmeyer, Moore prefers to paddle on both sides of the boat, changing hands to keep the boat tracking straight, or to turn it. This is accomplished with great speed and dexterity. Cajuns, on the other hand, preferred a longer paddle and invariably paddled on the same side of the boat all the time, using a J-stroke to

keep the craft going straight. [13] While fishing,
Moore sculls with the paddle using one hand,
thus freeing the other hand to control the fishing rod. When jump-shooting (or "bushwhacking") ducks, he has devised a special two-
paddle strategy. One paddle is in hand, another
carried in the boat. When he jumps a duck, he
drops the paddle he is using without any con-
cern about where it falls, which is usually in
the water. Then, after grabbing his gun and
shooting the duck, he uses the second paddle
to retrieve both the downed duck and the first
paddle. For the business of jump-shooting
ducks in heavy timber, Moore contends that
the split-second saved by dropping the paddle
makes a significant difference.

As late as the 1950's, fishermen and hunters
still liked the bateau for use on Caddo, but
they would tie it to the back of a motorboat
and tow it to the fishing or hunting grounds,
then anchor the motorboat and get into the
bateau to hunt or fish. Today, Caddo Lake is
mostly traveled by motorboats—some of them
remarkably large, considering the maze-like
nature of the Texas end of the lake, with its
labyrinthine channels, cypress "islands," and
endless meadows of lily pads. The motorboats
roar about in their narrow (and well-marked)
boat trails, or make short excursions into the
nearby swamp, leaving vast portions of the
area untraveled by man.

That is, unless the man should have a
bateau! The Caddo Lake bateau originally
evolved to meet these special circumstances,
and as a swamp boat it seems almost without
parallel. With its narrow waterline, it paddles
easily and with good speed. The flat bottom
and the low center of gravity of the bateau's
paddler ensure stability, and the flat, rockered
bottom means that the boat can be spun around
by a paddle sweep almost as easily as a white-
water kayak. This bottom slides easily over
water vegetation—a trait that can be fully ap-
preciated only by someone who has actually

13. Knipmeyer, "Folk Boats of Eastern French
Louisiana," p. 124.

tried to navigate in the frustrating world of the swamp, where the natural boundaries between land and water often seem to disappear, being replaced by a third element, which has characteristics of both. On the occasional stretches of extensive open water that are also typical of Caddo Lake (the "lakes" within the lake), the rockered ends of the bateau allow it to ride over big waves instead of plunging wetly through them, and the flaired sides turn aside waves coming in from abeam, making the boat remarkably seaworthy.

Moore and his bateau are still capable of venturing where few others could go. As he says, "The old-time fishing boat was a tool of the trade, and was designed to fit that purpose." As an ingenious folk technology for exploring the watery resources of the Caddo Lake swamplands, Moore's bateau works as well as it ever did.

Wyatt Moore tests the yet unpainted bateau on the waters of Caddo Lake, May 29, 1983.

Caddo Lake /
A Suggested Reading List

Biographical and Historical Memoirs of Northwest Louisiana. Nashville: Southern Publishing Co., 1890.

Campbell, Randolph B. *A Southern Community in Crisis: Harrison County, Texas, 1850–1880.* Austin: Texas State Historical Association, 1983.

Carruth, Viola. *Caddo: 1,000, A History of the Shreveport Area from the Time of the Caddo Indians to the 1970's.* Shreveport, La.: Shreveport Magazine, 1971.

Dahmer, Fred. "Caddo Was." 6 chapters. *Greater Caddo Lake Association News*, vols. 2 (June 1980), 3 (August 1980), 4 (October 1980), 5 (December 1980), 6 (February 1981), 7 (April 1981).

Dorsey, Florence L. *Master of the Mississippi, Henry Shreve, and the Conquest of the Mississippi.* Boston: Houghton Mifflin, 1941.

Dorsey, George A. *Traditions of the Caddo.* Washington, D.C.: Carnegie Institution of Washington, 1905.

Gleason, Mildred A. *Caddo.* Jefferson: Marion County Historical Commission, 1982.

Hackney, V. H. *Port Caddo—A Vanished Village and Vignettes of Harrison County.* Marshall, Tex.: Marshall National Bank, 1966.

Hardin, J. Fair. *Northwestern Louisiana: A History of the Watershed of the Red River, 1714–1937.* 3 vols. Shreveport, La.: Historical Record Association, 1938.

Hope, Alonzo P. *A Legend of Caddo Lake.* Edited by V. H. Hackney. Marshall, Tex.: Marshall National Bank, 1965.

Kirkland, Elithe Hamilton. *Love Is a Wild Assault.* Garden City, N.Y.: Doubleday and Co., 1959. (Fictionalized account of the story of Harriet and Robert Potter.)

McClung, Mildred Mays. "Caddo Lake—Moss-Draped Swampland of Mystery." Thesis, East Texas State University, 1955.

———. *Caddo Lake, Mysterious Swampland.* Texarkana: Southwest Printers and Publishers, 1974.

McLure, Mary Lilla and Howe J., eds. *History of Shreveport and Shreveport Builders*. Shreveport, La.: Journal Printing Co., 1937–1951.

Smith, Frank D. "Caddo Lake." Unpublished paper. Caddo Lake Oral History Project, East Texas State University, Commerce.

Tarpley, Fred. *Jefferson: Riverport to the Southwest*. Austin: Eakin Press, 1983.

Tyson, Carl Newton. *The Red River in Southwestern History*. Norman: University of Oklahoma Press, 1981.

Index